THE TRUE ENTREPRENEURIAL ATTITUDE

Prof. Marcão – Marcus Vinícius Pinto

The True Entrepreneurial Attitude

© Copyright 2024- All rights reserved.

The information provided herein is stated to be true and consistent, wherein any liability, in terms of inattention or otherwise, for any use or abuse of any policies, processes or guidance contained herein is the sole and absolute responsibility of the reader.

Under no circumstances shall any legal liability or fault be maintained against the authors for any repair, damage or monetary loss due to the information contained herein, whether directly or indirectly.

The authors own all copyrights to this work.

Legal Issues

This book is copyrighted. This is for personal use only. You may not alter, distribute, or sell any part or the contents of this book without the consent of the authors or copyright owner. If this is violated, legal action may be initiated.

The information contained herein is offered for informational purposes only and is therefore universal. The presentation of the information is without contract or any kind of warranty.

The trademarks that are used in this book are used for examples or composition of arguments. This use is done without any consent, and the publication of the trademark is without permission or endorsement from the trademark owner and are the property of the owners themselves, not affiliated herewith.

The images that are present here without authorship citation are public domain images or were created by the authors of the book.

Disclaimer.

Please note that the information contained in this document is for educational and entertainment purposes only. Every effort has been made to provide complete, accurate, up-to-date and reliable information. No warranty of any kind is express or implied.

By reading this text, the reader agrees that under no circumstances are the authors liable for any losses, direct or indirect, incurred as a result of the use of the information contained in this book, including, but not limited to, errors, omissions, or inaccuracies.

ISBN.

Selo editorial. Independently published

Summary

1 CAN YOU TELL WHAT IT'S LIKE TO BE A PERSONAL ENTREPRENEUR?................23

1.1 THE PERSONAL ENTREPRENEUR. 25

1.2 EXAMPLES OF SUCCESSFUL ENTREPRENEURS...28

1.3 THE MOTIVATIONS OF SUCCESSFUL ENTREPRENEURS..30

2 THE ENTREPRENEURIAL ATTITUDE. 33

2.1 WHY DO YOU NEED ENTREPRENEURIAL ATTITUDES? 33

2.2 WHAT ARE THE ATTITUDES THAT DEFINE A SUCCESSFUL ENTREPRENEUR? 35

2.2.1 Passion. 36

2.2.2 Courage...37

2.2.3 Flexibility/Adaptability..38

2.2.4 Ethics...39

2.2.5 Integrity. 40

2.2.6 Realistic approach. 40

2.2.7 Focus on the customer. 40

2.2.8 Creativity. 41

2.2.9 Nitpicking. 41

2.2.10	Vision.	42
2.2.11	Leadership.	43
2.2.12	Communication.	45
2.2.13	Self-motivation.	45
2.2.14	Awareness of your limits.	46
2.2.15	Technical proficiency.	46
2.2.16	Patience and Resilience.	46

3 THE ENTREPRENEUR IS NOT BORN READY. 49

3.1 Thoughts from great entrepreneurs. 50

3.2 Entrepreneurs must be able to pivot. 53

4 WHEN YOUR COMPANY IS YOURSELF. 57

5 WHY IS IT EASIER TO BE MANAGED THAN TO MANAGE? 64

5.1 When to be managed. 66

5.2 The banality of evil. 67

6 SOFT SKILLS NEEDED TO MANAGE YOUR LIFE. 71

6.1 Self-management. 71

6.2 Proactivity. 72

6.3 Resilience. 73

6.4 Effective communication. 75

6.5	CRITICAL THINKING.	77
6.6	EMPATHY AND EMOTIONAL INTELLIGENCE.	78
6.7	ADAPTABILITY.	82
6.8	LEADERSHIP.	85
6.9	HONESTY AND INTEGRITY.	86
6.10	TROUBLESHOOTING.	87
6.11	COLLABORATION.	88
6.12	NON-VERBAL COMMUNICATION.	90
6.13	PERSUASION.	92
6.14	CREATIVE THINKING.	93
6.15	CONFLICT MANAGEMENT.	94
6.16	FLEXIBILITY.	95
6.17	TIME MANAGEMENT.	96
6.18	MINDFULNESS.	97
6.19	NETWORKING.	98
6.20	SELF-MOTIVATION.	100
6.21	CULTURAL ADAPTABILITY.	101
6.22	OPENNESS TO CONTINUOUS LEARNING.	102
6.23	EMPATIA DIGITAL.	104

6.24	Emotional resilience.	105
7	**BURNOUT OF PROFESSIONALS.**	**109**
7.1	How far will you go to achieve and sustain success?	116
7.2	Symptoms of burnout.	118
7.2.1	Do co-workers become your enemies?	119
7.2.2	Do you have Monday panic?	119
7.2.3	Is your life a life sentence without parole?	120
7.2.4	Are shiny new opportunities always catching your eye?	120
7.2.5	Is LinkedIn the terror of your existence?	121
7.3	These clues can prevent burnout from setting in.	122
8	**SUICIDE FOR PROFESSIONAL REASONS.**	**125**
8.1	Factors for a suicide for professional reasons.	127
8.2	Suicide due to job loss.	128
8.3	KAROSHI.	132
9	**A NORMOSE.**	**137**
10	**PROFESSIONAL EXPECTATIONS AND FRUSTRATIONS.**	**146**
11	**IN SEARCH OF LOST RECOGNITION.**	**151**
11.1	The lack of recognition.	151

11.2	THE LACK OF RECOGNITION FROM CUSTOMERS.	153
12	**THE SECRETS TO HAVING A TRUE ENTREPRENEURIAL ATTITUDE.**	**158**
12.1	VISION AND INNOVATION.	158
12.2	2. DETERMINATION AND PERSISTENCE.	159
12.3	LEARNING CAPACITY.	159
12.4	NETWORKING AND COLLABORATION.	161
12.5	FOCUS AND PLANNING.	163
12.6	COURAGE AND RISK-TAKING.	166
12.7	ETHICS AND INTEGRITY.	168
12.8	PASSION AND PURPOSE.	169
13	**CONCLUSION.**	**174**
14	**REFERENCES.**	**178**
16	**MEET THE AUTHOR.**	**185**
16.1	PROF. MARCÃO - MARCUS VINÍCIUS PINTO.	185
16.2	SOME BOOKS PUBLISHED BY PROF. MARCÃO.	187
16.3	HOW TO CONTACT PROF. MARCÃO.	190

The True Entrepreneurial Attitude

Figures

Figure 1 – Being responsible for your ventures is a challenge. _____ 18

Figure 2 – Personal entrepreneurship. _____ 25

Figure 3 – Examples of successful entrepreneurs. _____ 29

Figure 4 – Knowing how to be an entrepreneur is a talent to be developed. _____ 31

Figure 5 – What does it take? _____ 33

Figure 6 – Courage. _____ 37

Figure 7 – Flexibility at work. _____ 38

Figure 8 – Ethics. _____ 39

Figure 9 – Focus on the customer. _____ 41

Figure 10 – Nitpicking. _____ 42

Figure 11 – Leadership. _____ 43

Figure 12 – Harry S. Truman. _____ 44

Figure 13 – Self-motivation. _____ 45

Figure 14 – Resilience. _____ 47

Figure 15 – That is the question! _____ 49

Figure 16 – Team spirit. _____ 51

Figure 17 – Limitless ideas. _____ 52

Figure 18 – Knowing when to pivot is crucial for success. _____ 54

Figure 19 - J.K. Rowling. _____ 60

Figure 20 – Ricardo Amorim. _____ 61

Figure 21 – Managed or manage? _____ 64

Figure 22 – Hannah Arendt. _____ 66

Figure 23 – Self-management. _____ 71

Figure 24 – Resilience. _____ 73

Figure 25 - Stephen Covey _____ 74

Figure 26 – Components of effective communication. _____ 75

Figure 27 - Dale Carnegie. _____ 76

Figure 28 – Peter Drucker _____ 78

Figure 29 – Daniel Goleman. _____ 79

Figure 30 – Empathy. _____ 80

Figure 31 – David Caruso. _____ 81

Figure 32 – John Cotter _____ 83

Figure 33 – Brian Tracy. _____ 83

Figure 34 – Adaptability. _____ 84

Figure 35 – Leadership. _____ 85

Figure 36 – Collaboration. _____ 89

Figure 37 – Non-verbal communication. _____ 91

Figure 38 – Conflict management. _____ 95

Figure 39 – Emotional resilience. _____ 105

Figure 40 - Herbert J. Freudenberger. _____ 110

Figure 41 - ChristinaMaslach. _____ 111

Figure 42 - Maslach Burnout Inventory. _____ 112

Figure 43 –Burnout. _____ 115

Figure 44 "It may be a slow burn, but at the limit we have a real explosion. _____ 117

Figure 45 – It's amazing how you don't notice the symptoms of burnout!_____ 118

Figure 46 – Alison Miller, Matthew J. Spital, Jane Pirkis at Anthony de Lamontagne _____ 126

Figure 47 - Vítima do Karoshi. _____ 133

Figure 48- Normosis?_____ 138

Figure 49 – Children's normose. _____ 139

Figure 50 - Jean-Yves Leloup. _____ 142

Figure 51 - Pierre Weil. _____ 142

Figure 52 - Roberto Crema. _____ 143

Figure 53 - Viktor Frankl. _____ 147

Figure 54 – Lack of professional recognition. _____ 152

Figure 55 – Lack of recognition from customers. _____ 155

Figure 56 – An endless climb with no guarantees. _____ 174

Figure 57 – Some books by Prof. Marcão. _____ 187

Figure 58 – Some more books by Prof. Marcão_____ 188

Figure 59 - Books on Open Data by Prof. Marcão. _____ *189*

Figure 60 – Let's value teachers. _____ *191*

To my beloved Andrea,

that may not always be right,

But he's always right.

Prof. Marcão – Marcus Vinícius Pinto

WELCOME.

"Entrepreneurship is not for everyone" – many of us have heard this warning coming from friends, family and even the whispering voices of our most hidden fears.

Whether or not we agree with this adage, one conclusion is incontrovertible:

> *Entrepreneurship really isn't easy! Challenges are numerous, and the statistics can be discouraging.*

However, despite the evident adversities, a growing number of individuals choose to take the path of entrepreneurship, with the aim of transforming their lives and their careers.

Taking the reins of your professional career as an entrepreneur offers the unique opportunity to crystallize your most audacious dreams. You start to shape your products and strategies, forging them in the fire of your own purpose, envisioning a professional reality that resonates with your inner ideals.

This path is not trodden in search of guarantees; rather, it is paved by a spirit of adventure and an acceptance of uncertainty. Everyday heroes don't launch themselves on the entrepreneurial journey only attracted by the glimmer of potential success; They also understand that every failure carries with it the germ of wisdom and strengthening.

Success and failure, in their whims, offer no certainties, but promise one thing: learning.

Figure 1 – Being responsible for your ventures is a challenge.

For the bold protagonists of their own business careers, the rewards far outweigh financial metrics. It's about personal fulfillment, the satisfaction of seeing an enterprise born of your aspirations take shape and impact the world in a positive and meaningful way. And even though the waves of uncertainty loom threatening, it is in the braving of these waters that the true learning lies.

Entrepreneurship is, in essence, a narrative of self-discovery and courage. And if you're considering becoming the author of your own business story, remember that the pages are blank, waiting for the ideas that only you can conceive of and the actions that only you can take.

Dedicate yourself to the venture with determination and resilience, study the market and learn from those who have already walked similar paths. The search for knowledge is constant; So have good reads and be open to absorbing valuable lessons from each experience. Good learnings become your best asset, empowering you to make informed choices and adapt to the rapidly evolving business world.

As you navigate the odyssey of entrepreneurship, there will be many ups and downs, but it is the passion for what you do and the conviction in your purpose that will be the driving winds that keep you going. Don't forget that the most valuable rewards often come after the biggest challenges. So, cultivate patience, sustain persistence, and celebrate every little step forward on the path to realizing your entrepreneurial dream.

Look at each new day as another chance to grow, to innovate and, above all, to build a legacy that inspires others to follow in your footsteps. The entrepreneur's journey is both personal and universal – you're not only building a business, but you're also forging an example of possibility and perseverance.

Be prepared to be a perpetual student, an intrepid problem solver, and above all, the architect of your own career. Good readings and excellent learning await you on this exciting journey called entrepreneurship.

Prof. Marcão - Marcus Vinícius Pinto
Digital Influencer
Entrepreneurship Specialist, Soft Skills,
product pricing and neuromarketing.
Founder, CEO, teacher and pedagogical advisor of
MVP Consult.

The True Entrepreneurial Attitude

"The great secret of life is that there is no great secret. Whatever your goal is, you can get there if you're willing to put in the work."

Oprah Winfrey

The True Entrepreneurial Attitude

1 CAN YOU TELL WHAT IT'S LIKE TO BE A PERSONAL ENTREPRENEUR?

Being an entrepreneur is more than being a business owner, it's a perspective and a lifestyle.

The path to personal entrepreneurship is often treacherous, full of unexpected detours, obstacles, and dead ends. There are too many sleepless nights, plans that don't work out, financing that doesn't arrive, and clients that never materialize. Launching a business can be so challenging that it can make you wonder why anyone would voluntarily go down this path.

Despite these difficulties, every year thousands of people embark on an entrepreneurial journey, determined to realize their vision and fill a need they see in society. They start brick-and-mortar businesses, launch tech startups, or turn an idea into a new product or service. With the right motivation, inspiration, and game plan, you too can be a successful entrepreneur.

An entrepreneur identifies a need that no existing company meets and determines a solution to that need.

Entrepreneurial activity includes developing and starting a new business and implementing a business marketing plan, often with the ultimate goal of selling the company for profit.

An entrepreneur who regularly launches new businesses, sells them, and then starts new companies is a serial entrepreneur. Whether an entrepreneur should be considered an entrepreneur often depends on whether they created the business and other legalities. That said, any successful family business founder started out as an entrepreneur.

If you want to become an entrepreneur but worry that you won't have the money to do so, finances don't have to stop you from achieving your career goals.

Many entrepreneurs seek funding options that bypass traditional banks, such as funding from angel investors that provide entrepreneurs with capital to cover startup costs (or, later, expansion costs).

If you can demonstrate a high growth potential for your business, you can also turn to a venture capitalist, who offers capital in exchange for part of your company.

All professionals—doctors, lawyers, engineers, and accountants—undergo rigorous training and education to master their respective fields. This is also true for professional entrepreneurs.

Think about it.

- Would you like the professional designing your home to be doing this as their first project outside of school?
- How about having your appendix removed by a newly minted doctor doing your first surgery?

In both scenarios you can get lucky, but do we want to rely on luck in these situations, or on skill and experience? The same goes for setting up a business.

Most colleges and universities offer basic and advanced business courses designed to teach both general and traditional concepts. However, even though these courses are necessary to learn the fundamental principles of business, they do not teach you how to be an entrepreneur.

They only provide a roadmap. You also need to develop skills and acquire specific knowledge in practice if you seek to excel as an entrepreneur.

Experience is the best teacher. It always has been and always will be. Observe how things are done, right or wrong, then experiment on your own. That's the secret of all learning.

1.1 The personal entrepreneur.

A personal entrepreneur, who can be a self-employed professional, is someone who applies the principles of entrepreneurship to managing their own career, regardless of whether they are leading a startup, freelancing, or navigating the dynamics of a large corporation.

This type of entrepreneurship is focused on forging a career path that reflects the individual's personal vision, values, and goals. The hallmark of the personal entrepreneur's performance is proactivity: instead of waiting for opportunities to present themselves, he creates them.

Figure 2 – Personal entrepreneurship.

The challenges faced by the personal entrepreneur are multifaceted. First, there is the challenge of self-motivation. Unlike a traditional employee, the personal entrepreneur often needs to set and maintain their own pace of work and continually seek opportunities for advancement and development. This also includes the challenge of being resilient in the face of failure or subpar returns.

Another significant challenge is building a strong personal brand. The impression that others have of a professional can open or close doors. Therefore, the personal entrepreneur must strive to create a reputation that is aligned with their career goals, using social networks, networking, and other visibility strategies.

Efficient management of time and resources is also critical. The personal entrepreneur needs to prioritize value-adding activities and discard what is superfluous or distracting. Additionally, the challenge of work-life balance cannot be ignored, especially for those who run their own businesses or are self-employed.

To overcome these challenges, there are several applicable strategies:

1. Set clear goals. Having a clear set of professional and personal goals can help you stay focused and motivated. It is important to set short-, medium-, and long-term goals that are SMART (Specific, Measurable, Attainable, Relevant, and Time-bound). By visualizing where they want to go, the personal entrepreneur can build a strategic path and adjust it as needed.

2. Develop a Strong Personal Brand. Invest time in developing and communicating your personal brand. This involves being aware of your public image, your skills, and how you can differentiate yourself in your field. Being authentic and consistent with your online and offline presence is key to building credibility and attracting business or career opportunities.

3. Learn continuously. Continuous skill development is a must. The personal entrepreneur must be willing to educate themselves, whether through formal courses, readings, workshops, or other forms of learning. Adaptability is a competitive advantage in today's rapidly changing job market.

4. Expand your network. Networking is crucial. Building and maintaining a network of contacts can lead to fruitful collaborations, new clients, or jobs. Attending industry events, engaging in online groups, and staying active in professional communities are all ways to expand your network.

5. Cultivate resilience. Developing a thick skin and a positive attitude in the face of failures and rejections is important. Learn from mistakes and see them as stepping stones to success. Having resilience also means knowing when it's time to change direction or adjust goals to adapt to new circumstances.

6. Manage Your Time and Resources Efficiently. Learn to say "no" to projects that don't align with your goals. Use time management tools and techniques to maximize productivity and ensure that you are allocating your resources—including time, money, and energy—in a way that benefits your long-term goals.

7. Maintain Work-Life Balance. It is vital for the personal entrepreneur to be mindful of their own physical and mental health. Set clear boundaries between work and play, and make sure to make time for rest, hobbies, and social life. Balancing these aspects not only increases professional effectiveness, but also prevents burnout and keeps motivation high.

8. Find a Mentor or Coach. Having a mentor or coach can be one of the most impactful decisions for personal and professional growth. This person can offer guidance, support, and valuable feedback based on their own experience and success. Counseling can help you see blind spots in your work and accelerate your development.

9. Use technology to your advantage. Technology can be a great ally of the personal entrepreneur when it comes to organization, efficiency, and accessibility to information. Project management tools, productivity apps, and online learning platforms are just a few examples of how technology can increase the ability to achieve professional goals.

10. Evaluate and Adjust Regularly. Self-knowledge is key to successful personal entrepreneurship. Regularly evaluate your progress against your goals and be willing to adjust as your experiences and the environment around you evolve. This may mean the need to recalibrate objectives, change strategies, or acquire new skills.

11. Prepare for Risks. Self-entrepreneurship often involves taking calculated risks. This does not mean acting recklessly, but having the courage to make thoughtful and timely decisions, even in the face of uncertainty. Evaluate the possible scenarios and have a contingency plan for each risk situation.

Being a personal entrepreneur means seeing yourself as a company that is constantly improving and innovating. It's about approaching every new opportunity and challenge with a strategic mindset and long-term vision.

Success in this area goes beyond accomplishing tasks and achieving financial goals; It is a journey of self-development, in which the individual is both the catalyst and the beneficiary of continuous progress.

When embarking on the journey of personal entrepreneurship, it's also crucial to recognize the importance of emotional well-being. The pressure to succeed can be intense, and without the proper support, one can easily fall into traps like burnout and isolation. That's why it's essential to build a solid support network, whether it's through colleagues, friends, family, or mental health professionals.

Also important is the ability to celebrate victories, both big and small. Every step forward is a success to be recognized and celebrated. This celebration not only strengthens the momentum to move forward, but also adds joy and satisfaction to the experience of personal entrepreneurship.

1.2 Examples of successful entrepreneurs.

Many people whose names no one knew decades ago exemplify entrepreneurial success today. Here are some examples.

- ❖ Steve Jobs. The late tech leader started Apple in a garage and built it into the dominant company it is today. Jobs even faltered in the middle of his career, leaving Apple for more than a decade before returning to the company and taking it to new heights.
- ❖ Elon Musk. He founded SpaceX and has since become known for investing the billions of dollars his company has earned him in some benevolent

projects, including providing clean drinking water to Flint, Michigan, and donating FDA-approved ventilators to hospitals battling COVID-19.

Figure 3 – Examples of successful entrepreneurs.

- ❖ Bill Gates. The Microsoft co-founder has often been listed as the world's richest individual and has become an internationally renowned leader on pandemics and how to deal with them. The Bill & Melinda Gates Foundation, shared with his ex-wife, focuses on fighting poverty, inequality and disease globally.
- ❖ Jeff Bezos. The founder and creator of Amazon.com originally started the company as an online book retailer. Since then, the internet marketplace has become one of the most valued companies in the world, selling almost every product imaginable.
- ❖ Mark Zuckerberg. As a college student, he helped shape the future of social media by co-founding the social networking platform Facebook. Initially

launched only to select college campuses, the service quickly expanded to the general public. His success has turned Zuckerberg into one of America's youngest billionaires.

- ❖ Sara Blakely. She took $5,000 and turned it into a $1 billion company with an invention known today as Spanx. The idea was born out of Blakely's frustration with the pantyhose she had to wear in previous jobs. She had no experience in fashion, but she researched everything from patents to fabrics.

1.3   The motivations of successful entrepreneurs.

What motivates entrepreneurs to venture out when so many others would run in the opposite direction? While everyone's inspiration is different and unique, many entrepreneurs are spurred on by one or more of the following motivators.

1. Autonomy. Entrepreneurs are people who want to be their own bosses, set their own goals, track their own progress, and run their businesses as they see fit. They recognize that the success or failure of their business depends on them, but they don't see this responsibility as a burden. Instead, they see it as a marker of their freedom.
2. Goal. Many entrepreneurs have a clear vision of what they want to accomplish and will work tirelessly to make it happen. They truly believe they have a product or service that fills a gap, and they are compelled by a single-minded commitment to keep moving forward. They hate stagnation and would rather fail as they move forward than languish in inactivity.
3. Flexibility. Not everyone fits the rigidity of traditional corporate culture. Entrepreneurs often seek to break free from these constraints, find a better work-life balance, or work at times and in unconventional ways. That doesn't mean they're working fewer hours — often, especially in the early stages of growing a business, they work harder and harder — but instead, they're working in a way that's instinctive to them.

Figure 4 – Knowing how to be an entrepreneur is a talent to be developed.

4. Financial success. Most entrepreneurs realize that they won't be billionaires overnight, but that doesn't mean they aren't interested in the potential of making a lot of money from a hugely successful business that they have complete control over. Some want to establish a financial safety net for themselves and their families, while others are looking to make a huge profit by creating the next big thing.
5. Legacy. Entrepreneurs are often driven by the desire to create something that outlasts them. Others want to develop a brand that has longevity and becomes an institution. Some want to pass on a source of income and security to their heirs. There are also entrepreneurs who hope to make a lasting impression on the world and leave a legacy of innovation that improves people's lives in some tangible way.

"Opportunities don't arise. You're the one who creates them."

Chris Grosser[1]

---

[1] Grosser pioneered freelancing platform Upwork and cloud computing company Digital Ocean.

2 THE ENTREPRENEURIAL ATTITUDE.

If you're considering becoming an entrepreneur, first identify which of the above motivators serve as your guiding forces.

Next, consider whether you possess the specific character traits and attributes that will allow you to thrive as an entrepreneur.

Figure 5 – What does it take?

Do you have what it takes to be a self-employed entrepreneur?

Do you have the entrepreneurial spirit in you?

2.1   Why do you need entrepreneurial attitudes?

As an entrepreneur, you need these entrepreneurial attitudes as they enhance your chances of success.

The True Entrepreneurial Attitude

The combination of the right attitude and mindset is one of the fundamental keys to success in business.

The combination of the right attitude and mindset is one of the fundamental keys to success in business. The way we face challenges, deal with adversity, and stay focused on our goals can determine the direction and magnitude of our achievements in the entrepreneurial world.

Having the right attitude means having determination, resilience, and optimism in the face of obstacles that come your way. It is the ability not to be overwhelmed by difficulties, to persist even when things seem difficult, and to see opportunities where others see only problems. A positive attitude is contagious and inspiring, motivating not only yourself but also those around you.

The right mindset, on the other hand, involves the ability to think strategically, creatively, and innovatively. It is the ability to analyze situations from different perspectives, identify innovative solutions and anticipate market trends. A growth-oriented mindset and continuous learning is essential for staying competitive and relevant in the ever-evolving business world.

When we combine a positive attitude with a success-oriented mindset, we are able to overcome challenges, explore new opportunities, and reach higher and higher levels in our entrepreneurial journey. Confidence, resilience, creativity, and the ability to adapt quickly to change become our greatest allies in the pursuit of business success.

In addition, the combination of the right attitude and mindset allows us to maintain emotional balance in the face of the pressures and uncertainties of the business world, making assertive decisions and staying focused on our long-term goals. Clarity of purpose, discipline, and the ability to deal with uncertainty are essential aspects of building a strong and lasting foundation for success in business.

Importantly, the combination of the right attitude and mindset is not a static attribute, but rather a skill that can be developed and improved over time. The practice of self-awareness, self-knowledge and self-development are fundamental

to cultivate a positive and proactive attitude in the face of the challenges that arise in the business world.

Additionally, pursuing constant learning, being open to new ideas and experiences, and surrounding yourself with inspiring and motivating people are also effective strategies for strengthening the right attitude and mindset combination. Networking, mentoring, and participating in events and training programs are valuable opportunities to expand horizons, acquire new knowledge, and build relationships that drive professional and personal growth.

All in all, the combination of the right attitude and mindset is a powerful lever for success in business, as it empowers us to take on challenges, explore opportunities, and achieve our goals with determination, creativity, and resilience. By cultivating a positive, confident, and innovation-driven attitude, we are not only building a strong foundation for success in our endeavors, but also inspiring and motivating those around us to achieve their best selves.

Therefore, you need to develop a positive entrepreneurial attitude if you want to achieve success in business.

- ✓ A creative mindset helps businesses succeed.
- ✓ With new ideas, it's easier for you to take your business to the desired level.
- ✓ Attitude is one of the factors that distinguishes one person from another. Thus, an entrepreneurial attitude will distinguish you from other entrepreneurs.
- ✓ When this entrepreneurial attitude becomes a part of you, it spreads to other areas of your life making you a better person overall.

2.2 What are the attitudes that define a successful entrepreneur?

Being a professional with an attitude is essential in all segments of the corporate world. And this is even more essential when it comes to entrepreneurs, as they need the right attitude to start and run a successful business.

Entrepreneurial attitudes are behavioral traits that can help an entrepreneur grow and succeed in business. Without them, it can be challenging to grow your business.

Moreover, it is these attitudes that will allow an individual to set up and run a business effectively.

Here are some entrepreneurial attitudes you need if you want to succeed in business.

2.2.1   Passion.

One of the attributes that an entrepreneur must possess is passion.

Passion is often a driving force that can help entrepreneurs stay in business regardless of the challenges they face.

A passionate entrepreneur will, in most cases, have the right motivation to build their business successfully.

Most entrepreneurs move very fast because of the passion they have for their idea and company.

In addition, some entrepreneurs derive pleasure from knowing that they have what it takes to put smiles on people's faces.

They are problem solvers, and as an entrepreneur, you should make your work your passion. Motivation for success is what leads to passion.

With passion, an entrepreneur can effectively create new business ideas or improve an existing product.

2.2.2 Courage.

Just like every human being with fear, entrepreneurs are afraid of failing in their goals, but they don't allow fear to be a factor that prevents them from achieving their goals.

Figure 6 –Courage.

Most entrepreneurs have failed before, but instead of backing down, they use failure to their advantage. And instead of stopping, they move forward to succeed.

They seek to ensure success the next time they try the same idea.

In other words, the fear of failure motivates them to work harder and achieve success in their goals.

Bravery and courage define entrepreneurs. These attributes work together.

Being in charge requires a great deal of courage from the entrepreneur to take on any task correctly without anyone helping them.

Most entrepreneurs give their best in the face of difficult situations and this makes their confidence a direct result of the results obtained.

2.2.3   Flexibility/Adaptability.

Most entrepreneurs face obstacles, but unlike others, entrepreneurs who have a high degree of flexibility/adaptability deal with these setbacks differently.

Figure 7 – Flexibility at work.

Having flexibility and adaptability prevents them from feeling discouraged when problems arise on their way to success.

This makes them open-minded to change and are more likely to see ways to solve problems.

As a result, help them progress.

2.2.4 Ethics.

Ethics is an essential attribute for entrepreneurs. Starting a business from scratch requires you to work hard for long hours.

Winning for the sake of winning, without scruples, without ethics, does not generate the results expected by entrepreneurs who are truly successful.

Figure 8 –Ethics.

He keeps in mind that every decision he makes should consider the needs of his customers.

Entrepreneurs, in most cases, live for their customers, just as doctors exist for the sake of their patients.

2.2.5 Integrity.

Honesty and truthfulness should not be lacking in an entrepreneur.

An entrepreneur must show their customers that you possess these qualities by being honest and trustworthy in your business of dealing with them.

The business in which he is involved should not prevent him from having integrity.

If your customer asks for products or services, make sure you deliver them in the way they need to.

This will prove to your customer that you are reliable and trustworthy.

2.2.6 Realistic approach.

Entrepreneurs see and accept things the way they really are.

Entrepreneurs are eager to know the state of a certain problem at every moment.

In addition, entrepreneurs are always connected with the news because it keeps them informed about what they need to know.

Before making any decisions, they do in-depth research and analysis to determine their feasibility.

2.2.7 Focus on the customer.

Entrepreneurs value and respect their customers. That's because they clearly understand the role of customers in business. Without customers, no business can exist.

Figure 9 – Focus on the customer.

Therefore, they are always customer-oriented in business.

2.2.8   Creativity.

Entrepreneurs have unique creative ideas, they are innovative in their approach to thinking.

Creativity is one of the most essential things that are needed to build a successful business. With a creative mindset, an entrepreneur can transform an existing product into something unique and better.

Above all, passion and creativity are keys to building businesses.

2.2.9   Nitpicking.

Successful entrepreneurs are very observant and alert. They understand that difficult situations require them to plan and develop various business ideas.

Figure 10 –Nitpicking.

They see possibilities faster than others and are always alert for information and facts that are essential to your business.

Entrepreneurs examine all the possibilities needed to achieve their goals and devote their strength to completing a task immediately.

2.2.10 Vision.

Most entrepreneurs start their businesses because they find them challenging. Thus, they give everything it takes to make the business work.

Visionary entrepreneurs have the right approach to how the business should work. This allows them to put the right resources in the right places so that their vision is confirmed.

2.2.11 Leadership.

Entrepreneurs are excellent leaders. They know how to lead people and their business without difficulties.

Figure 11 –Leadership.

They are very good at bringing people and their businesses together.

Good leadership involves several other attitudes and skills such as communication, ethics, and courage. In business, it's invariably tied to performance, whether it's profit or results.

And as Harry Truman said,

> "Leadership is the ability to get people to do what they don't want to do and enjoy doing it."

Figure 12 – Harry S. Truman[2].

---

[2] Harry Truman was the 33rd President of the United States, serving from 1945 to 1953, following the death of Franklin D. Roosevelt. He became head of state during the final months of World War II and made crucial decisions that influenced the global stage, including the controversial use of nuclear weapons against Japan to end the war. He also implemented the Marshall Plan to rebuild Europe after the war and established the Truman Doctrine, marking the beginning of the Cold War with the Soviet Union.

2.2.12 Communication.

This attitude is essential for entrepreneurs to communicate effectively with their customers and employees.

Successful communication happens when the message is clearly conveyed and understood.

Entrepreneurs with excellent communication skills are likely to stand out more than those who don't.

2.2.13 Self-motivation.

Like passion, self-motivation is another strong factor for success in entrepreneurship.

This is what fuels the efforts that entrepreneurs put into the business.

Figure 13 – Self-motivation.

Without motivation, entrepreneurs will give up on their business goals at the slightest touch of challenges and obstacles.

2.2.14 Awareness of your limits.

Of course, an entrepreneur needs to put in a lot of effort to succeed in the business, but it is necessary to set real and achievable goals.

Conscience in this case even considers the physical limits of the entrepreneur.

Without having these boundaries well defined, it will be impossible to stay on track and achieve success.

2.2.15 Technical proficiency.

Technical skills are very important to have as an entrepreneur.

It may seem difficult to achieve, but it is essential.

You can take the time and learn the skills you need for efficiency and productivity in your business.

2.2.16 Patience and Resilience.

These attitudes are also mindsets and, at the same time, essential attitudes that most successful entrepreneurs have.

They can withstand challenging times and setbacks in their business. Not because they like failures, but because they've trained themselves not to give in to challenging situations.

In addition, they learned not to allow difficult circumstances around them to determine their fate.

Figure 14 –Resilience.

However, resilience and patience don't happen overnight. It takes practice and commitment to build the mental toughness to endure hardship.

Overall, an entrepreneur is a leader, creative, reliable, competent, and has technical skills, etc.

They have a better chance of succeeding in business than those without these attributes mentioned above.

"*Always be thinking about how you can do better.*"

ELON MUSK

3 THE ENTREPRENEUR IS NOT BORN READY.

There is no one-size-fits-all path to becoming a successful entrepreneur. A lot of it can come down to having the right skills, mindset, and ideas at the right time to resonate with the audience. However, there are a few things you can do to increase your chances of starting a thriving business.

Find the right idea. Entrepreneurship isn't just about finding a profitable idea, it's about finding one that you're passionate about pursuing. Almost every industry has room for new entrepreneurs, and identifying the subject you care about most can motivate you to stay the course.

Figure 15 – That is the question!

Develop a plan for your business. It's not enough to say you want to start a business, you also need a solid plan for how to do it. A business plan can help solidify the financial goals you want to achieve. It can also tell you how to reach them while attracting potential investors to fund your venture.

Determine your clientele. Not many businesses become successful without serving customers. Most ventures won't appeal to all members of the public equally, but you can gauge interest in your idea before you open your doors. The demographics of the people who are most interested in your business can help you make other decisions, such as the location of your store and ad purchases.

Sell your idea. Even if your product or service has piqued the interest of friends, family, or online forums, this is a small sample. You need to have a sense of what the audience thinks. Getting your idea out there in the right places and highlighting what sets it apart from competitors can help attract people to your business.

Get to know others in your field. Chances are, there are people in your industry whose expertise in certain areas can benefit your fledgling business. A proper network can connect you with people from whom you can gain valuable knowledge or get monetary support. Instagram business accounts are worth following to learn from peers and experts.

3.1 Thoughts from great entrepreneurs.

To help you determine if you have what it takes, here are 9 thoughts from high achievers who bring entrepreneurial attitudes closer to us.

1. Entrepreneurship is at the heart of many professionals' dreams. It's about breaking new ground, believing in yourself, your mission, and inspiring others to join you on the journey. What sets entrepreneurs apart is the willingness, courage, and sometimes recklessness to actually do it.
2. The most successful entrepreneurs are those who possess drive. They are made up of persistence, passion, and resilience. It's the passion to achieve long-term goals, the courage to try again in the face of rejection, and the will to do something better than what's been done before. The most successful entrepreneurs tend to be brave... They don't give up until they exceed their goals. When the going gets tough and they get knocked down, brave entrepreneurs bounce back and try again.

3. The ability to listen, whether it's the opinions of customers or employees, is also essential for success. While you should have the confidence to make your own choices, it's still incredibly important not to let go of the people whose needs you're trying to meet.

Figure 16 – Team spirit.

4. Being a successful entrepreneur also means being a good leader. Leadership is the ability to get people to a place where they want to follow you, not feel forced to follow you. This leads to investing in your team personally. They should know that you will not only hold them accountable and push them to be better, but also take care of them when they are struggling. It's not transactional, it's a relationship.
5. Being an entrepreneur is like stepping into uncharted territory. It's rarely obvious what to do next, and you have to rely a lot on yourself when you run into problems. There are many days when you feel like things are never going to work out and you're trading at a loss for endless months. You have to be able to endure the rollercoaster of emotions that comes with fighting on your own.

6. Entrepreneurs need to be people-oriented. Your business will die without a good team to support it. Study management techniques, learn from great leaders, and review where you're succeeding and failing so you can help others improve. An entrepreneur has to be able to build a team that cares about their work, and for that, you need to care about how you build your team.

Figure 17 – Limitless ideas.

7. To be a successful entrepreneur, you need perseverance. Most successful business owners or entrepreneurs have never given up on their idea. When challenges arise, they find innovative ways to overcome them. You must be able to adapt to changing economic conditions, innovate, and embrace technological advancements to keep your customers engaged. These things require determination and a strong focus on the end goal.
8. Successful entrepreneurs look beyond the obvious and instead look at the bigger picture to ensure that every action taken is going toward the overall goal of the business or concept, whether or not that means getting something in return at that moment.

9. Being an entrepreneur is rooted in one's identity. It's the culmination of a certain set of characteristics. determination, creativity, risk-taking, leadership and enthusiasm.

3.2 Entrepreneurs must be able to pivot.

Entrepreneurs are often celebrated for their business acumen and courage to tread uncharted territory. What really challenges and defines an entrepreneur, however, is not just the ability to launch an audacious idea, but rather the ability to adapt and evolve in the face of adversity and changes in the landscape.

The art of pivoting—that is, the ability to fundamentally alter direction when the current path proves fruitless—is a vital tool in the belt of any agile business.

Insisting on a strategy that has been proven not to yield the expected results is like trying to make a plant grow without sunlight – useless, if not harmful. In such cases, persistence gives way to inflexibility, a trait that rarely correlates to business success. By contrast, the willingness to reassess, and, if necessary, reformulate business approaches and models, is the true power of dynamic entrepreneurship.

Pivoting doesn't mean hastily abandoning a plan at the first sign of challenge; It's a strategic shift informed by market feedback, performance reviews, and often experience-forged intuition.

This power of adaptation does more than just avoid failure; It reveals new avenues and opportunities that may not have been initially visible.

Being adaptable implies a constant willingness to learn and a recognized humility that allows the entrepreneur to understand that the market is an entity in constant mutation.

In the face of anything that is 'thrown' at them – be it an economic crisis, the emergence of a disruptive technology, or a change in consumer behaviors and preferences – the flexible entrepreneur is the one who can stay on their feet, accurately assessing the situation and implementing quick and effective changes.

Figure 18 – Knowing when to pivot is crucial for success.

To fully embrace the pivot philosophy, the entrepreneur must always be attentive to market signals and willing to question their own assumptions. This requires a combination of vigilance and critical thinking that can identify when a change of course is not just a possibility, but a necessity.

In many cases, this decision may involve exploring new products, redefining the target audience, changing sales channels, or even completely transforming the business model.

The key to a successful pivot lies in the ability to carry it out in a sustainable and calculated manner. This means carefully planning the transition, ensuring that resources are reallocated efficiently and that the team is aligned and prepared for the upcoming changes.

Setting up performance indicators to monitor the progress of the new strategy is also critical to ensure that the pivot is moving in the desired direction.

However, the power of the pivot lies not only in the strategic change, but also in the mindset of the entrepreneur. Developing a company culture that values flexibility, innovation, and resilience can turn a simple trajectory adjustment into a propellant to new heights of success.

Cultivating a mindset that sees challenges as opportunities and failures as lessons, rather than defeats, gives entrepreneurs and their teams the confidence to navigate the uncertainties of entrepreneurship.

In an increasingly fast-paced and unpredictable business world, the ability to pivot becomes one of the most essential and distinctive qualities of the successful entrepreneur. In essence, to be adaptable is to recognize that the entrepreneurial journey is a continuous learning process, where every setback is an invitation to innovation, and every change, a step towards a brighter and more promising future.

The entrepreneur who masters the power of the pivot is the one who, regardless of the obstacles, stays the course toward the realization of his highest goals and aspirations.

In addition, the act of pivoting requires from the entrepreneur not only a strategic vision, but also interpersonal skills and effective leadership. Clear and persuasive communication becomes imperative to ensure that the entire team understands and embarks on the new direction. The leader should be the beacon that guides through periods of uncertainty, conveying confidence and showing how the new directions align with the company's long-term vision.

Entrepreneurs also need to develop the ability to make decisions with agility, but without haste. Quickly assessing the risks and benefits, consulting with mentors, industry experts, and reliable data are all practices that help identify the right time to pivot, as well as the most promising measures to implement.

In this way, the entrepreneur who effectively appropriates the power of the pivot navigates today's dynamic entrepreneurial ecosystem not only as a mere participant, but as a pioneer capable of responding, reinventing, and reconfiguring its journey toward sustainable and meaningful triumph.

"I'm successful today because I had a friend who believed in me and I didn't have the courage to let him down."

Abraham Lincoln

4   WHEN YOUR COMPANY IS YOURSELF.

When the company is the person themselves, that is, when it comes to the career of an entrepreneurial, freelancer, self-employed or independent professional, the challenges are many and varied.

Managing one's own career as if it were a company requires specific skills, autonomy, proactivity, and the ability to adapt to the changes and challenges of the labor market.

Let's take a look at some of the most common challenges faced by those who are responsible for managing and directing their own career.

1. Self-management. In a traditional company, there are managers, supervisors, and leaders who guide, supervise, and direct the activities of employees. However, when the person is the company itself, it is necessary to develop self-management skills, such as time organization, setting goals and objectives, setting priorities, and strategic planning. The ability to self-manage effectively is essential for achieving career success.
2. Uncertainty and instability. The career of an independent professional or entrepreneur is subject to uncertainty and instability, since there are no guarantees of continued employment, fixed salary, or traditional benefits. Dealing with the unpredictability of the market, the variation in demand for services, and the lack of job security are constant challenges for those who are the company itself.
3. Skills development. To remain competitive and relevant in the job market, it is essential to constantly invest in the development of skills and competencies. Learning new technologies, enhancing technical knowledge, developing interpersonal and leadership skills, and staying up-to-date with industry trends are all essential aspects for individual career success.
4. Networking and personal marketing. Building a solid network, prospecting for new business opportunities, promoting personal services and skills, and developing a strong personal brand are all determining factors for individual career success. Networking and personal marketing play a crucial role in

generating new opportunities, attracting clients, winning strategic partnerships, and expanding professional reach.

5. Financial management. Managing personal and business finances efficiently is one of the biggest challenges for those who are the company itself. It is necessary to have control over costs, set competitive prices, prepare budgets, ensure cash flow, and plan investments strategically to ensure the financial health of the individual career in the long term.

6. Work-life balance. The lack of separation between personal and professional life is a common challenge for those who are responsible for managing their own career. The need to always be available, to work flexible hours, and to deal with the constant pressure for results can affect work-life balance, which can lead to stress, exhaustion, and compromised physical and mental health.

7. Maintaining motivation and focus. Maintaining motivation and discipline throughout the professional journey can be a challenge, especially in the face of the ups and downs of the job market, the difficulties and obstacles faced. It is essential to cultivate self-discipline, resilience, and determination to overcome difficult times, stay focused on goals, and persist towards individual career success.

8. Time and priority management. Balancing the various demands and responsibilities of an individual's career, such as performing day-to-day tasks, developing new projects, attracting clients, and conducting networking activities, requires advanced time management and priority management skills. Knowing how to identify what is most important and urgent, setting a realistic timeline, and setting achievable goals are essential aspects of optimizing productivity and ensuring individual career success.

Managing one's own career as if it were a company is a complex challenge that requires specific skills, autonomy, proactivity and adaptability. Dealing with market uncertainty and instability, constantly developing skills, building a solid network, managing finances efficiently, balancing personal and professional life, maintaining motivation and focus, and managing time and priorities are just some of the challenges faced by those who are responsible for the direction and success of their own career.

However, by developing these skills and adopting a posture of self-management and leadership, it is possible to overcome challenges and achieve success in one's individual career. With determination, perseverance, and commitment, it is possible to transform one's personal career into a journey of professional growth, fulfillment, and success.

In this context, there are several success stories of individuals who knew how to masterfully manage their careers, achieving professional recognition, financial success and personal fulfillment. Let's take a look at some of these inspiring cases:

1. Camila Coutinho. The Brazilian digital influencer and businesswoman is known for being one of the pioneers in influencer marketing in the country. Camila Coutinho created the blog "Garotas Estúpidas" in 2006 and has since built a powerful personal brand, expanding her business into areas such as fashion, beauty, lifestyle and style consulting. Its ability to undertake, innovate and adapt to market trends has made it one of the main success stories in the Brazilian digital market.
2. Cristiano Ronaldo. Although he is Portuguese, footballer Cristiano Ronaldo is also an inspiring success story in managing his own career in Brazil. Ronaldo is recognized as one of the greatest athletes in the history of the sport, winning titles, awards, and records throughout his career. In addition to his undoubted talent as a player, Ronaldo also invests in his own businesses, such as hotels, restaurants, and fashion brands, demonstrating his entrepreneurial vision and ability to diversify his sources of income.
3. Elon Musk. The South African entrepreneur is known for being the founder and CEO of innovative companies such as Tesla, SpaceX, and Neuralink. Musk manages his career in a visionary way, betting on high-impact projects and investing in disruptive technologies that have the potential to transform the world. Her ability to take risks, think innovatively, and lead with determination is an inspiring example for anyone who wants to successfully manage their career.
4. J.K. Rowling. The author of the "Harry Potter" book series is a striking example of success in managing her own career. J.K. Rowling began her career writing the story of the young wizard in cafes in Edinburgh, Scotland,

and faced several rejections from publishers before having her first book published. With determination, creativity, and commitment, she has built a literary empire that has become one of the most popular and profitable franchises in history.

Figure 19- J.K. Rowling.

5. Luiza Helena Trajano. The Brazilian businesswoman is one of the main examples of success in career management in Brazil. Luiza Helena Trajano is Chairman of the Board of Directors of Magazine Luiza and was instrumental in transforming the company into one of the largest retailers in the country. His entrepreneurial vision, dedication, commitment, and leadership skills have contributed significantly to the growth and success of the business.
6. Marie Forleo. The entrepreneur, author, and MarieTV presenter is known for helping people build successful businesses and careers aligned with her values and purpose. Marie Forleo has built a multi-million dollar platform based on her commitment to personal empowerment, creativity, and authenticity. Her ability to manage her own career in a way that aligns with her values and passions is an inspiring example for those seeking professional and personal success.

7. Ricardo Amorim. The Brazilian economist and entrepreneur is known for his work as a speaker, consultant and host of television programs. Ricardo Amorim is a reference in economics and finance in the country, and is frequently invited to discuss relevant topics about the financial market and the Brazilian economic scenario. In addition to his career as an economist, Amorim is also an entrepreneur, investor, and book author, demonstrating his ability to successfully manage a multifaceted and impactful career.

Figure 20 – Ricardo Amorim.

8. Rodrigo Faro. The Brazilian presenter and entrepreneur is another example of success in managing his own career. Rodrigo Faro has built a solid career in television, standing out for his versatility, charisma and talent. In addition to his successful career in the media, Faro also invests in his own ventures, diversifying his sources of income and consolidating his image as a successful and respected professional.
9. Sara Blakely. The founder of the lingerie company Spanx is another example of success in managing her own career. With just $5,000 in savings and an innovative idea, Sara Blakely revolutionized the women's underwear market and built a billion-dollar empire. Her determination, entrepreneurial vision

and ability to identify the needs of the market were fundamental to the success of her professional career.
10. Tim Ferriss. The American author and investor is known for his innovative approach to work and career. Tim Ferriss is a proponent of the concept of "remote work" and efficient productivity, having written bestsellers such as "Work 4 Hours a Week" and "Work Less, Produce More." Her ability to manage her own career in a flexible, adaptable and results-focused way is an inspiring example for those who seek to achieve professional success with balance and efficiency.

These are just a few examples of Brazilian success stories in managing their own careers, which demonstrate the importance of self-management, strategic vision, discipline and determination to achieve professional success.

Each of these professionals has built a trajectory of excellence and impact, inspiring others to follow in their footsteps and seek personal and professional development.

"The banality of evil lies in the absence of thought."

Hannah Arendt

5 WHY IS IT EASIER TO BE MANAGED THAN TO MANAGE?

The phrase "Because it's easier to be managed than to manage" raises profound questions about the dynamics of power, control, and responsibility present in leadership and subordinate relationships.

This question reflects the perception that taking on the role of leadership and management entails a series of challenges and responsibilities that are often perceived as more complex and demanding than simply following the guidance and direction of a leader or manager.

Figure 21 – Managed or manage?

Being managed involves following instructions, meeting deadlines and set goals, and receiving feedback and guidance on the work done. In this role, the individual can feel more secure and comfortable since they don't have to deal with the pressure of making difficult decisions, facing conflict, or taking responsibility for the performance and results of a team or project.

On the other hand, managing implies making decisions, delegating tasks, motivating and guiding a team, resolving conflicts, dealing with the demands and expectations of superiors and employees, and taking responsibility for the success or failure of the work performed.

These responsibilities require leadership, communication, problem-solving, and time management skills, as well as the ability to handle pressure, stress, and uncertainty effectively.

The difficulty in assuming the role of manager or leader can be attributed to a number of factors, such as fear of failure, lack of confidence in one's own abilities and competencies, pressure for results, the need to deal with complex and challenging situations, and exposure to constant criticism and evaluation.

Many people prefer to avoid these uncomfortable situations and choose to follow the directives and guidance of a superior, even if it means giving up the autonomy, creativity, and personal and professional development that can come from exercising leadership and management.

However, it is important to note that taking on the role of a manager entails numerous opportunities for growth, learning, and fulfillment. Being an effective leader requires communication, empathy, decision-making, and conflict management skills, as well as the ability to inspire and motivate team members, foster a healthy and productive work environment, and achieve organizational objectives and goals effectively.

Despite the challenges and responsibilities of the role of a manager, many people find great satisfaction and fulfillment in taking on this role, as it provides the opportunity to positively influence people's lives, develop leadership and management skills, and contribute to the growth and success of the team and the organization as a whole. Additionally, being a good manager can open doors to new

career opportunities, professional recognition, and personal and professional growth.

5.1   When to be managed.

The question "Why is it easier to be managed than to manage?" refers to a deep reflection on the dynamics of power, authority and responsibility in social and organizational relations, from the perspective of Hannah Arendt's philosophy and work, especially considering her book "Eichmann in Jerusalem. The Banality of Evil," which addresses ethical and political issues related to totalitarian regimes and the acts of banality that allowed the Holocaust to occur.

Figure 22 – Hannah Arendt.

From Arendt's point of view, the notion of the banality of evil refers to people's ability to commit terrible and inhumane acts passively, without thinking critically about the consequences of their actions, simply following orders and directives from higher authorities, without questioning or reflecting on the morality and ethics involved.

In this context, being managed can represent uncritical adherence to a higher authority, passive acceptance of orders and directives, and a lack of critical engagement and personal responsibility for the consequences of one's actions.

Arendt highlights the importance of individual responsibility and the ability to think critically and act autonomously in the face of complex and challenging situations. Being managed, in this sense, can be easier than managing, as it involves following instructions, complying with established norms and rules, and abdicating, to some extent, the autonomy and freedom of thought and action that are essential to assuming the role of leader and manager.

Taking on the role of manager entails making difficult decisions, dealing with conflicts, taking responsibility for a team's performance and results, and facing the uncertainties and challenges inherent in exercising leadership. These responsibilities require capabilities such as critical thinking, ethics, effective communication, empathy, and thoughtful decision-making, which can be quite complex and challenging to develop and exercise effectively.

5.2   The banality of evil.

In the context of the banality of evil, the question of being managed or managing also refers to the ethical and moral dimension of power and authority relations. The idea of blindly following orders and directives from a higher authority, without questioning or reflecting on the justice and morality of such actions, can lead to situations where the person becomes a mere instrument in the hands of an oppressive and inhumane power structure, contributing to the perpetuation of injustices and atrocities.

Arendt highlights the importance of individual responsibility and the ability to act autonomously and consciously, taking responsibility for one's choices and actions, and resisting conformity and passive submission in the face of arbitrary and tyrannical authorities. In this sense, being managed can represent a state of alienation and annulment of individual responsibility, while managing implies assuming one's own agency and autonomy, and acting ethically and responsibly in the face of the demands and challenges of the contemporary world.

Thus, by traversing Hannah Arendt's reflections on the banality of evil and the ethical and political issues involved in passive submission to the orders of a higher authority, the question about the ease of being managed in relation to the challenge of managing acquires a deeper and more complex dimension.

Being managed can represent a form of evasion of responsibility and autonomy, a passive acceptance of established power structures, while managing entails taking one's own agency, thinking critically, acting ethically and responsibly, and assuming the consequences of one's actions and choices.

In this way, the question of why it is easier to be managed than to manage, in the light of Hannah Arendt's philosophy and her reflection on the banality of evil, invites us to reflect on the complex dynamics of power, authority and responsibility that permeate human and organizational relationships, and on the importance of autonomy. critical thinking and ethical and responsible action as foundations for building a more just, free and democratic society.

Through reading and reflecting on works such as "Eichmann in Jerusalem. The Banality of Evil", we are challenged to question the structures of power and authority that shape our lives, to take a critical and active stance in the face of the injustices and oppressions of the contemporary world, and to seek ways to act ethically and responsibly, resisting conformity and passive submission to the orders and directives of arbitrary and inhumane authorities.

Thus, when faced with the question of the ease of being managed in relation to the challenge of managing, it is important to consider the teachings and reflections of

Hannah Arendt's philosophy, which invites us to think about the complex relations of power, responsibility, and autonomy that permeate social and organizational interactions.

Being managed can represent a form of alienation and annulment of individual responsibility, while managing implies assuming one's own agency, acting consciously and ethically, and resisting the pressures and injustices of the contemporary world, in search of a more authentic, meaningful, and worthy life to be lived.

"Soft skills, such as empathy, communication, and adaptability, pave the personal entrepreneur's path to success, because leadership is not just what we do, but how we relate to others along our path."

Simon Sinek[3]

---

[3] Author known for his works on leadership and motivation

6 SOFT SKILLS NEEDED TO MANAGE YOUR LIFE.

To be responsible for your professional life, it is essential to possess a series of "soft skills" or behavioral skills that go beyond technical knowledge and specific job-related skills.

These skills are essential for effectively managing your career, dealing with challenges, and achieving your professional goals. Here are some of the key soft skills you'll need to take responsibility for your work life.

6.1   Self-management.

Effective time and resource management is key in the professional environment. As Peter Drucker, considered the father of modern management, stated, "Efficiency is doing the right things; Effectiveness is about doing the right things."

Figure 23 –Self-management.

This entails setting clear and prioritized goals, as highlighted by Stephen Covey in his book "The 7 Habits of Highly Effective People." "Start with the end in mind."

By prioritizing tasks and organizing work according to these goals, it is possible to achieve high-quality results, as advocated by Brian Tracy, renowned author and personal development speaker, who emphasizes. "Success is achieved by doubling down on your efforts, not reducing your goals."

Staying focused on what's really important is essential to avoid wasting time and energy. As mentioned by Jim Rohn, author and entrepreneur famous for his teachings on leadership and self-improvement, "Success is doing what you want, when you want, where you want, with who you want, for as long as you want."

The ability to manage your time, energy, and resources effectively and efficiently is a key differentiator for achieving professional success.

6.2   Proactivity.

The ability to be proactive in your career, as highlighted by renowned management thinkers, is crucial to professional success. Stephen Covey, author of "The 7 Habits of Highly Effective People," points out that "talent is a gift, but skill is a choice. Be proactive." This statement reinforces the importance of taking responsibility and acting proactively to achieve your goals.

Peter Drucker, considered the father of modern management, also addresses the importance of proactivity when he states that "the best way to predict the future is to create it". In other words, by taking the initiative and acting oriented towards growth and continuous improvement, you have the power to shape your own professional destiny.

Constantly seeking opportunities for growth and development is key to staying relevant in the ever-changing job market. As Warren Bennis, a renowned theorist of leadership, argued, "The only thing that is certain about the future is that it will be different. Be open and ready to grow and evolve." This underscores the importance of being proactive in seeking feedback, constant learning, and improving your skills and knowledge.

Taking initiative in your career, rather than passively waiting for opportunities, is essential to achieving success and realizing your full potential. As quoted by Brian Tracy, renowned author and personal development speaker, "The only thing that separates you from what you want in life is the willingness to try and the faith that it is possible to achieve." Therefore, being proactive is more than an attitude, it is a mindset that drives excellence and enables professional and personal growth in a continuous and meaningful way.

6.3   Resilience.

Resilience, as highlighted by renowned management thinkers, plays a key role in the ability to cope with pressure, stress, and challenges constructively and positively. In his words, renowned author and speaker Tony Robbins emphasizes that "The true measure of success is how you deal with failure." This reflects the importance of being resilient and learning from adversity, turning challenges into opportunities for growth.

Figure 24 –Resilience.

Peter Drucker, considered one of the greatest thinkers in management, also addresses resilience in his work, stating that "the best way to predict the future is to create it."

This perspective highlights the importance of adapting to change, overcoming obstacles, and maintaining a positive attitude in the face of difficulties, as an essential part of the process of building a successful professional future.

Another influential thinker, Stephen Covey, author of the book "The 7 Habits of Highly Effective People," highlights the importance of adopting a proactive mindset in overcoming challenges. According to Covey, "You are the creator of your own reality." This statement underscores the power of resilience and a positive attitude in shaping the path to success, even in the face of adverse situations.

Figure 25 - Stephen Covey

Resilience is not limited to overcoming momentary difficulties, but rather to cultivating a continuous ability to adapt and overcome. As quoted by John Maxwell, author and leadership expert, "Resilience is not just having the ability to bounce back from an obstacle, but also to evolve, adapt, and change in the face of adversity."

Therefore, being resilient is more than simply resisting adversity, it is moving towards personal and professional growth and transformation.

6.4   Effective communication.

The ability to express yourself clearly, assertively, and confidently is widely recognized as key to taking responsibility for your professional life. Renowned management thinkers emphasize the importance of effective communication as a key competency in the workplace.

Figure 26 – Components of effective communication.

As quoted by Peter Drucker, known as the father of modern management, "Communication is the essence of management." This statement highlights the crucial role that communication plays in interaction within an organization, underscoring the importance of conveying messages clearly and assertively in order to achieve positive results.

Covey emphasizes the importance of "First seek to understand, then be understood," highlighting the need to listen carefully and communicate clearly and assertively in order to establish strong and productive relationships.

According to Dale Carnegie, a renowned author in the field of personal development and interpersonal relationships, "Language is a garment for action." This quote underscores the importance of utilizing communication as a tool to express your ideas, needs, and expectations effectively, positively influencing how you are perceived and how your messages are received.

Figure 27 - Dale Carnegie.

Therefore, by developing the ability to communicate clearly, assertively, and confidently, you will strengthen your professional relationships, resolve conflicts constructively, and collaborate productively with colleagues and superiors. Taking responsibility for your professional life includes enhancing effective communication as an essential tool for success and continued development in your career.

6.5   Critical thinking.

The ability to analyze information, evaluate options, make informed decisions, and solve problems effectively is essential to taking responsibility for your professional life. Renowned management thinkers highlight the importance of critical thinking as a crucial competency for success in the corporate environment.

Peter Drucker, known as the guru of modern management, underscored the relevance of critical thinking by stating that "management is about doing the right things; Leadership is about doing the right things." This quote highlights the need to discern situations, identify effective solutions, and make informed decisions in order to achieve desired outcomes.

Making informed decisions and solving problems effectively requires the ability to evaluate information objectively. As Warren Bennis, a renowned author and leadership expert, pointed out, "Successful leaders adapt to unexpected changes and anticipate challenges." This underscores the importance of developing critical thinking skills to deal with ambiguity and uncertainty wisely.

The ability to identify creative solutions is also a valuable critical thinking skill. Stephen Covey, a renowned author and personal effectiveness expert, emphasized the importance of "starting with the end in mind." This approach underscores the need to visualize desired outcomes and find innovative avenues to achieve them through careful and unbiased analysis.

Figure 28 – Peter Drucker

By cultivating critical thinking, you will be able to analyze clearly, evaluate objectively, and make informed decisions in your professional life. Taking responsibility for your career requires the continuous development of this skill in order to face challenges with confidence, identify opportunities for growth, and achieve your goals consistently and effectively.

6.6   Empathy and emotional intelligence.

The ability to understand and manage emotions, both your own and those of others, is an essential skill for taking responsibility for your professional life. Recognized management thinkers emphasize the importance of emotional intelligence and empathy in the workplace, as a fundamental foundation for establishing meaningful relationships and fostering a collaborative and empathetic environment.

Daniel Goleman, a renowned author and psychologist, popularized the concept of emotional intelligence, highlighting it as crucial for success in both professional and personal life.

Goleman points out that "empathy is one of the greatest emotional and social skills that each of us possesses. It's what allows us to sincerely share the joy and pain of others." This quote underlines the importance of empathy in building authentic connections and healthy relationships in the workplace.

Figure 29 – Daniel Goleman.

On the other hand, Adam Grant, an expert in organizational psychology, highlights the importance of empathy for effective leadership. Grant states that "empathy is about leading with understanding. It's about perceiving the situation from the other's point of view, showing solidarity and encouragement."

This perspective underlines the crucial role of empathy in positively influencing others and fostering a productive and harmonious work environment.

Managing your own emotions and expressing them appropriately is an essential part of emotional intelligence. As stated by Brené Brown, researcher and best-selling author, "Vulnerability is the basis of all emotions and feelings."

Figure 30 –Empathy.

This underscores the importance of expressing authenticity and vulnerability in order to establish genuine connections and foster a healthy and inclusive work environment.

By developing emotional intelligence and cultivating empathy, you will strengthen your leadership skills, enhancing your interpersonal relationships and contributing to a positive and collaborative work environment.

Taking responsibility for your professional life requires the continuous practice of these skills in order to foster a healthy and productive organizational climate.

Acknowledging one's own emotions, as well as those of others, contributes to more effective communication, constructive conflict resolution, and the strengthening of bonds of trust and cooperation in the workplace.

In addition, emotional intelligence and empathy are key to dealing with stress, pressure, and challenging situations that are part of everyday work.

As pointed out by David Caruso, renowned psychologist and researcher, "Emotional intelligence is not a panacea. Emotional intelligence is about understanding human emotions and influences."

Figure 31 – David Caruso.

This highlights the importance of developing the ability to deal with emotions in a positive and constructive way, even in the face of complex and demanding scenarios.

Taking responsibility for your professional life therefore involves a commitment to honing your emotional intelligence and empathy in order to lead with compassion, positively influence those around you, and contribute to an inclusive and motivating work environment.

By cultivating these skills, you'll be not only strengthening your leadership and collaboration skills, but also building genuine and meaningful relationships that drive growth and success in your career path.

6.7   Adaptability.

The ability to adapt to ever-changing work environments is considered essential by renowned management thinkers. In an era of accelerated transformation, adaptability becomes a differentiator for professional success and the ability to assume responsibilities in different contexts.

One of the experts in change management, John Kotter, highlights the importance of adaptability by stating that "the winners are those who are able to adapt in an era of constant change".

This quote underscores the need to remain flexible and open to new possibilities in order to meet the challenges and take advantage of the opportunities that arise in the corporate environment.

Renowned author and speaker Brian Tracy also emphasizes the relevance of adaptability, stating that "the only constant in life is change."

Figure 32 – John Cotter

Figure 33 – Brian Tracy.

This finding reflects the reality of the business world, where the ability to learn new skills, adjust to new realities, and innovate becomes essential to remain relevant and competitive.

Developing the ability to adapt quickly to new situations not only allows you to deal with immediate challenges, but also makes it possible to take advantage of opportunities for professional growth and evolution.

As Charles Darwin points out, "it is not the strongest that survives, nor the most intelligent, but the one that best adapts to change." This maxim underscores the importance of adaptability as a key to survival and success in the ever-changing business environment.

Figure 34 –Adaptability.

Taking responsibility for your professional life includes a commitment to developing the ability to adapt, learn continuously, and adjust to change in an agile and assertive way. By cultivating adaptability, you will be prepared to face the challenges of the corporate world and leverage your career proactively and successfully.

6.8 Leadership.

The importance of leadership skills, even outside of formal management positions, is highlighted by renowned management thinkers. The ability to influence, inspire, collaborate in a team, resolve conflicts, and make decisions directly impacts the progress and success of one's professional career.

Warren Bennis, considered one of the greatest scholars of leadership, points out that "The ability to lead is to influence. The ability to influence is to lead." This statement highlights the essence of leadership. the ability to inspire and motivate others to achieve common goals, regardless of the position held.

Figure 35 –Leadership.

Simon Sinek, renowned author and speaker, highlights the importance of collaboration and conflict resolution for effective leadership. Sinek states that "Trust and collaboration are the keys to an effective team." This perspective emphasizes the need to build solid relationships, based on trust and teamwork, in order to achieve successful results in the professional environment.

Making correct decisions for the benefit of the group is also an essential skill for leading effectively, regardless of hierarchical position. As quoted by Dwight D. Eisenhower, "The best decisions are not necessarily the easiest." This quote highlights the importance of considering the well-being of the group and making strategic decisions, even in the face of complex challenges and dilemmas.

Taking responsibility for your career path includes a commitment to developing leadership skills, regardless of the position held. By cultivating the ability to influence, inspire, collaborate, and make decisions for the benefit of the group, you will not only be progressing your career but also contributing to fostering a collaborative and motivating work environment for all.

6.9   Honesty and Integrity.

Acting ethically and transparently in all professional interactions is a fundamental principle widely highlighted by renowned management thinkers. Building a solid and trustworthy reputation is based on honesty, integrity, and a commitment to ethical values, which are essential for success and excellence in the workplace.

Peter Drucker, considered the father of modern management, underscores the importance of business ethics by stating that "Any organization is not just a business structure; it is, first and foremost, an ethical framework." This statement highlights the central role of ethics and integrity in building trusting relationships and fostering a healthy and ethical work environment.

One of the experts in leadership and management, Stephen Covey, also emphasizes the relevance of integrity in professional interactions. Covey argues that "The mind is a garden in which values are planted." This illustrates the importance of cultivating ethical values, such as honesty and transparency, to ensure credibility and trust in personal and professional relationships.

In addition, Mahatma Gandhi, a pacifist leader and example of ethical conduct, underscores the importance of maintaining integrity in all circumstances. Gandhi stated that "Truth is never wrong, even if it seems utterly impracticable." This quote highlights the need to maintain coherence between words and actions, always acting with honesty and transparency, even in the face of challenges and pressures.

Taking responsibility for your ethical conduct and demonstrating integrity in your professional interactions not only strengthens your reputation but also builds foundation for long-lasting relationships of trust. By adopting ethical principles, you will not only be promoting an ethical and productive work environment, but also inspiring respect and admiration for your integrity and transparency in the corporate world.

6.10 Troubleshooting.

The ability to identify, analyze, and find effective solutions to challenges that arise throughout one's career is considered a valuable skill and widely recognized by renowned management thinkers. The ability to think creatively, collaborate effectively, and implement practical and feasible solutions is essential for overcoming obstacles and achieving professional success.

One of the most influential authors in the field of creativity, Mihaly Csikszentmihalyi, highlights the importance of creativity in solving complex problems. Csikszentmihalyi states that "Creativity results from an uninterrupted series of problem-solving." This underlines the need to think outside the box and find original solutions to stand out in the ever-evolving corporate environment.

In addition, renowned management consultant Peter Drucker emphasizes collaboration as an essential competency for professional success. Drucker states that "Collaboration is the ability to recognize the difference between interdependence and dependence, and to engender respect for that difference." In this way, the ability to work in a team collaboratively and respectfully is critical to effectively solving challenges and achieving positive results.

Henry Mintzberg, a renowned management theorist, highlights the importance of practical implementation of the solutions found. Mintzberg states that "Planning is fun, but the trivial is crucial." This quote highlights the importance of translating

creative ideas into concrete and feasible actions, in order to face the challenges of everyday life and achieve the proposed goals.

Taking responsibility for your ability to identify, analyze, and solve challenges throughout your career involves a commitment to creativity, collaboration, and the implementation of practical solutions. By cultivating these skills, you'll be prepared to face obstacles with confidence, find opportunities for growth, and establish a competitive edge in the job market.

Developing the ability to think creatively, work collaboratively, and implement effective solutions not only strengthens your professional skills but also demonstrates your proactivity and ability to adapt to the changes and challenges of today's work environment.

By investing in the improvement of these skills, you will be preparing yourself to face the increasingly complex and dynamic challenges of the business world, contributing to the growth and success of your professional journey. The ability to identify and solve challenges effectively is a differentiator valued by organizations and essential to stand out and progress in your career.

6.11   Collaboration.

The ability to work effectively in a team, collaborating with colleagues, superiors, and clients to achieve common goals, is critical to individual and organizational success.

Being collaborative entails several aspects, such as active listening, contributing constructive ideas, sharing knowledge and skills, and respecting the opinions and contributions of others. Collaboration is essential for fostering a harmonious work environment, stimulating innovation, and achieving exceptional results.

Renowned management scholars, such as Patrick Lencioni, highlight the importance of collaboration and teamwork for organizational success. Lencioni states that "Teamwork is the ability to work together towards a common vision.

It is the ability to direct individual accomplishments toward the goals of the organization." This perspective underscores the importance of joining forces towards a shared purpose, overcoming challenges and achieving meaningful results.

Figure 36 –Collaboration.

Peter Senge, a renowned author in the field of organizational learning, points out that "Organizations learn only through individuals who learn. Individual learning ceases to be useful, it results in a learning team." This statement underlines the importance of collaboration and knowledge exchange among team members to foster innovation, creativity, and collective development.

Taking responsibility for being an effective employee involves a commitment to contributing positively and constructively to collective success. By cultivating communication skills, empathy, and mutual respect, you will strengthen your interprofessional relationships, fostering a collaborative and participatory work environment, and driving excellence and innovation in the achievement of organizational projects and goals.

> *Collaboration is an essential pillar for long-term growth and prosperity for both individuals and organizations.*

6.12 Non-verbal communication.

Nonverbal communication plays a significant role in human interaction and is critical for effective communication in the workplace. In addition to verbal communication, the ability to understand and interpret body language, facial expressions, and gestures is essential for establishing bonds, conveying subtle emotions and messages, and strengthening professional relationships.

Renowned communication experts, such as Albert Mehrabian, point out that most human communication is non-verbal, consisting of elements such as tone of voice, gestures, posture, and facial expressions.

Mehrabian developed the so-called "7-38-55 Rule," which states that only 7% of communication is based on words, while 38% is based on tone of voice and 55% on body language. This illustrates the relevance of non-verbal communication in conveying messages and correctly interpreting communicative intentions.

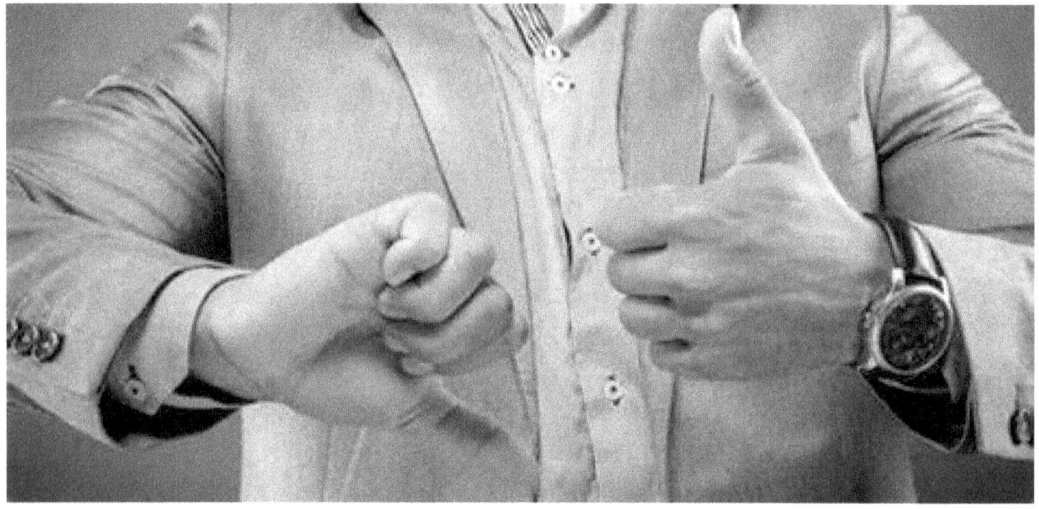

Figure 37 – Non-verbal communication.

The ability to understand the body language and non-verbal expressions of others is essential for correctly interpreting messages, establishing empathy, and building trusting relationships in the workplace.

Gestures such as maintaining eye contact, smiling, adopting an open posture, and using appropriate facial expressions can convey confidence, empathy, commitment, and assertiveness, positively impacting perception and interaction with colleagues, superiors, and customers.

Taking responsibility for enhancing your ability to interpret and utilize nonverbal communication effectively involves a commitment to developing sensitivity, empathy, and attention to detail in professional interactions.

By recognizing the importance of body language and facial expressions in communication, you will strengthen your communication skills, enhancing your ability to connect with others and building strong and productive relationships in the workplace.

Nonverbal communication is a powerful tool for conveying messages, establishing rapport and strengthening interpersonal communication.

By properly understanding and using body language and non-verbal expressions, you will be able to convey confidence, empathy, respect, and assertiveness, contributing to a more collaborative, harmonious, and productive work environment.

Additionally, nonverbal communication plays a crucial role in resolving conflicts, negotiating agreements, and leading teams. The ability to read the emotions and intentions behind facial expressions and gestures can help identify misunderstandings, create deeper connections, and foster a more inclusive and welcoming work environment.

Thus, taking responsibility for honing your nonverbal communication skills is essential for professional and personal development. By recognizing the importance of body language and nonverbal expressions in human interaction, you will invest in strengthening your interpersonal relationships, improving communication, and building a more positive and effective work environment.

Nonverbal communication is a powerful tool that, when used properly, can open doors to growth and success in your professional career.

6.13   Persuasion.

The ability to influence and persuade in an ethical and convincing manner is an essential and highly valued skill in any career. Persuasion involves presenting solid arguments, tailoring communication to the target audience, dealing with objections and resistance, and creating emotional and logical connections to gain the support and collaboration needed to achieve goals and objectives.

Renowned thinkers of communication and persuasion, such as Robert Cialdini, highlight the importance of principles such as reciprocity, authority, scarcity, consistency, commitment, and social approval in the ability to influence and persuade others effectively. By understanding these principles and applying them ethically, it is possible to increase your ability to influence and persuade in a variety of professional situations.

Ethical persuasion involves building solid and convincing arguments, based on facts and evidence, to gain the trust and credibility of the target audience. In addition, adapting communication to the profile and needs of the interlocutors, dealing empathetically and respectfully with objections and resistance, and creating emotional and logical connections are key strategies to promote persuasion effectively.

Taking responsibility for developing and honing your influencing and persuasion skills is critical to professional and personal success. By cultivating the ability to present compelling arguments, adapt communication strategically, and create meaningful connections with others, you will strengthen your ability to positively influence decisions, actions, and collaborations in the workplace and beyond.

Ethical persuasion is a powerful tool that, when used with integrity and skill, can open doors to new opportunities and contribute to your career growth and progress.

6.14   Creative thinking.

The ability to think innovatively, generate original ideas, and solve problems creatively is, in fact, essential to standing out and excelling in today's work environment. Creative thinking goes beyond the traditional way of approaching problems and challenges, encouraging the search for unconventional solutions, the generation of new opportunities, and the creation of value for both the organization and the individual himself.

Renowned innovation scholars, such as Steve Jobs and Elon Musk, highlight the importance of creative thinking and the search for original and disruptive solutions. Jobs stated that "Being creative means thinking differently, putting yourself in the spotlight, and stepping out of the box," while Musk, known for his visionary ideas and innovative projects, emphasizes the importance of seeking innovative and challenging solutions to the most complex problems.

Creative thinking is not just restricted to fields such as art and design, but is a valuable differentiator across all disciplines and professional sectors. It fosters the ability to see beyond the obvious, to connect seemingly unconnected ideas, and to find innovative solutions to everyday challenges and problems.

Taking responsibility for developing and cultivating the skill of creative thinking involves a willingness to explore new ideas, question the status quo, and experiment with new approaches. By investing in your ability to innovate and generate original ideas, you will not only be standing out in the workplace, but also contributing to personal and professional differentiation and progress.

Creative thinking is a powerful tool that can boost your career, promote innovation, and have a positive impact on your career path.

6.15　Conflict management.

Knowing how to deal with conflicts constructively is a crucial skill in the workplace, where interaction between people can lead to disagreements and disagreements.

Taking responsibility for managing conflict effectively involves the ability to identify the underlying causes, find balanced solutions, and promote open and effective communication between the parties involved.

The ability to deal with conflict constructively does not mean avoiding conflict or simply imposing solutions, but rather seeking to understand the different perspectives, interests, and needs of the parties and working together to identify solutions that meet everyone's interests. This requires empathy, active listening, communication skills, and a commitment to the peaceful resolution of differences.

Figure 38 – Conflict management.

Professionals who can manage conflict effectively contribute to promoting a healthy work environment in which employees feel heard, respected, and valued.

In addition, the ability to deal with conflicts in a constructive manner also assists in improving interpersonal relationships, strengthening trust, and establishing an organizational culture based on collaboration and open dialogue.

Taking responsibility for managing conflict effectively is critical for professional and personal development. By cultivating conflict resolution skills, you will strengthen your leadership capacity, improving the organizational climate and promoting productivity and satisfaction in the workplace.

The ability to manage conflict constructively is a skill valued by organizations and essential to take control of their professional life and contribute to a harmonious and effective work environment.

6.16   Flexibility.

In an ever-changing job market, the ability to adapt to new situations, embrace challenges, and take on new responsibilities is critical for professional success and career progression. Being flexible and adaptable allows you to quickly adjust to the demands of the work environment, cope with unexpected changes, and seize opportunities for growth and development.

The ability to adapt to new situations and embrace challenges is essential in a dynamic and competitive business landscape. Professionals who demonstrate flexibility and resilience are able to maintain productivity and performance even in the face of sudden changes, uncertainties, and external pressures, demonstrating essential skills to face the challenges of today's job market.

Taking responsibility for developing a flexible and adaptable posture involves cultivating skills such as the ability to constantly learn and reinvent oneself, the willingness to take risks and get out of one's comfort zone, and the willingness to face new challenges as opportunities for personal and professional growth and development.

Flexible professionals are valued by organizations for their ability to adapt quickly to ever-evolving work environments, contributing to innovation, creativity, and organizational success. Additionally, flexibility allows professionals to explore new possibilities, expand horizons, and achieve more ambitious goals and objectives, boosting career development and professional fulfillment.

Ultimately, flexibility is not just about the ability to deal with change, but also about the willingness to accept feedback, learn from mistakes, and proactively adapt to the new demands and challenges of the work environment.

By taking responsibility for developing the mindset and skills necessary to be flexible and adaptable, you will be preparing yourself to face the challenges of the job market successfully, promoting personal and professional growth and ensuring your relevance and success in an ever-evolving professional landscape.

Flexibility is a skill that is increasingly valued in today's job market and represents a competitive advantage for professionals looking to excel and thrive in their careers.

6.17   Time management.

Effectively managing time and tasks is of utmost importance for professional and personal success. The ability to prioritize activities, set realistic goals, avoid procrastination, and maintain a healthy work-life balance are key aspects of increasing productivity, reducing stress, and improving efficiency in meeting professional goals.

Time and task management is essential for optimizing performance and achieving desired results. When you are clear about priorities and take an organized approach to task execution, you can maximize effectiveness and efficiency, ensuring that each activity is completed properly and on time.

Avoiding procrastination and staying focused on the most important and urgent activities are key elements of effective time management. By creating a structured work routine, setting realistic goals, and aligning activities with professional objectives, it is possible to minimize distractions and optimize the use of time, ensuring that responsibilities are met more efficiently.

Additionally, maintaining a healthy work-life balance is essential for overall health and well-being. Overwork can lead to burnout and compromise quality of life, making it essential to make time for leisure, rest, and activities that provide emotional and physical well-being.

Taking responsibility for effectively managing time and tasks is an important step towards professional and personal success. By developing time management skills, task prioritization, and work-life balance, you will increase your productivity by reducing stress and improving your quality of life, contributing to achieving your goals and aspirations more effectively and satisfactorily.

Remember that time management is a skill that can be developed and improved over time, through consistent practices and the use of proper tools and techniques.

The key to effective time management lies in identifying key priorities, setting clear objectives, creating a detailed action plan, and maintaining focus and discipline in getting things done. With dedication and commitment, it is possible to achieve a healthy work-life balance, optimize productivity, and achieve the desired professional success.

6.18   Mindfulness.

Cultivating mindfulness and awareness of the present moment is a practice that can have numerous benefits for the workplace and life in general.

Mindfulness consists of being fully present and aware in the present moment, without judgment or distractions, which can significantly contribute to productivity, conscious decision-making, and stress reduction in the workplace.

Practicing mindfulness aids in the development of the ability to focus and concentrate, allowing you to fully engage in your activities and tasks, without getting carried away by distractions or worries. Increasing awareness of the present moment also fosters mental clarity and the ability to respond more appropriately and effectively to the demands and challenges of everyday life.

Additionally, mindfulness can be a powerful tool for dealing with stress and pressure in the workplace. By cultivating the ability to be present and mindful, it is possible to reduce anxiety, regulate emotions, and stay calm in the face of challenging situations, making it easier to cope with the stress and pressure of the work environment.

Taking responsibility for incorporating mindfulness practice into your daily routine can have significant benefits for your well-being and performance at work. By taking a few minutes out of your day to connect with yourself, cultivate mindfulness, and awareness of the present moment, you will strengthen your skills of concentration, mental clarity, and emotional resilience, contributing to greater efficiency, productivity, and satisfaction in the workplace.

Mindfulness not only benefits the individual, but it can also improve the organizational climate by fostering a culture of respect, empathy, and effective communication. By taking responsibility for practicing mindfulness and cultivating awareness of the present moment, you will invest in your mental and emotional health, improving your interpersonal relationships, and fostering a healthier and more productive work environment for yourself and others.

Mindfulness practice is a valuable tool for self-development, emotional balance, and professional success, and it can make a significant difference in your personal and professional life.

6.19   Networking.

Building and maintaining a network of professional contacts is an extremely important practice for career growth and success. Effective networking not only expands professional opportunities but also allows you to gain insights into the job

market, broaden influence in the professional environment, and create strategic partnerships that can drive professional development.

Having networking skills involves more than simply collecting contacts or handing out business cards. It's about establishing authentic connections, cultivating meaningful relationships, and knowing how to communicate effectively with different audiences. This requires empathy, interpersonal communication skills, the ability to listen actively, and a willingness to create genuine and lasting connections.

A solid network of contacts can offer several advantages, from the possibility of receiving referrals for job opportunities, to the chance to share knowledge and experiences with professionals from different fields. Additionally, effective networking can open doors to collaborations, joint projects, mentorship, and even new business partnerships.

Taking responsibility for cultivating a network of professional contacts requires dedication, consistency, and authenticity. Attending networking events, conferences, workshops, and professional meetups can provide opportunities to meet new people and expand your network. Additionally, utilizing online platforms, such as LinkedIn, to stay in touch with professionals you care about and share relevant content can be an effective strategy for strengthening your connections.

Investing time and energy into developing networking skills can be extremely beneficial for career growth and advancement. By taking responsibility for building and maintaining a solid professional network, you will be expanding your career opportunities, increasing your visibility in the job market, and strengthening your influence and credibility in the professional environment.

Remember that networking is a two-way street, so always be willing to collaborate, contribute, and add value to your contacts, creating mutually beneficial and lasting relationships. Building a solid network of professional contacts is a key strategy for professional success in an increasingly competitive and dynamic job market.

6.20 Self-motivation.

Having the ability to self-motivate and stay engaged and focused on your goals is key to taking responsibility for your professional life and achieving success. Self-motivation involves a series of skills and attitudes that drive us to pursue our goals with determination, commitment, and enthusiasm, even in the face of challenges and obstacles that may arise along the way.

To motivate yourself effectively, it is essential to set clear and specific goals that direct your actions and efforts towards achieving professional success. Setting challenging but achievable goals helps you stay focused and directed, and allows you to gauge your progress over time, which is key to maintaining motivation and determination.

In addition, self-motivation requires discipline, resilience, and persistence to overcome the difficulties and moments of discouragement that may arise throughout the professional journey. It's important to cultivate a positive mindset, learn from failures and setbacks, and find inspiration and internal motivation to keep moving towards your goals, even when things become challenging.

Finding sources of inspiration and motivation that resonate with your personal values, interests, and purposes can be instrumental in fanning the flame of self-motivation. This could involve seeking out successful role models, reading inspirational books, attending pep talks, or connecting with people who share your goals and worldview.

Taking responsibility for self-motivation and staying engaged in your professional life requires self-knowledge, self-discipline, and a commitment to yourself in pursuing your dreams and aspirations. By developing the ability to self-motivate, you will be strengthening your ability to overcome challenges, achieve your goals, and take the reins of your career in a proactive and determined way.

Remember that self-motivation is an essential quality for professional and personal success, and a skill that can be developed and honed throughout life. By taking responsibility for your self-motivation, you'll build the foundation for a successful career, a more fulfilled life, and a promising future.

Self-motivation is the key to staying focused, determined, and resilient in the face of challenges and adversity, and to achieving your goals and achieving your dreams. So don't underestimate the power of self-motivation and commitment to yourself in achieving your best self and taking control of your professional and personal life.

6.21   Cultural adaptability.

In an increasingly globalized world, the ability to adapt to different cultural environments and deal with diversity is a valued and essential skill in the job market. Cultural adaptability encompasses the ability to understand and respect different cultural perspectives, communicate effectively with colleagues from diverse backgrounds, and collaborate respectfully and inclusively in multicultural contexts.

The ability to adapt to different cultures and contexts is critical in an increasingly diverse and interconnected job market. Cultural adaptability involves the ability to understand and respect cultural differences, recognize and value diverse ways of thinking and acting, and communicate sensitively and inclusively, creating a more collaborative and harmonious work environment.

Understanding and respecting different cultural perspectives is essential for establishing positive and productive relationships with colleagues, customers, and business partners from diverse backgrounds. This requires empathy, openness to learning about new cultures, willingness to question and deconstruct stereotypes, and flexibility to adapt to the differences and peculiarities of each cultural context.

Additionally, cultural adaptability involves cross-cultural communication skills, which are essential for ensuring effective communication and avoiding misunderstandings in multicultural contexts. This includes the ability to adapt your communication style, to be clear and direct without disrespecting cultural differences, and to express yourself in a respectful and inclusive way, taking into account the cultural sensitivities and norms of the interlocutors.

Collaborating in a respectful and inclusive way in multicultural contexts requires an attitude of openness, respect and genuine interest in cultural differences, as well as a willingness to learn from others and contribute constructively to teamwork. This involves promoting diversity, equity, and inclusion in the workplace, and creating an organizational climate where all voices are heard and valued, regardless of their cultural background.

Taking responsibility for developing the skill of cultural adaptability is critical to professional success in an increasingly globalized and diverse world. By learning to understand, respect, and communicate effectively in multicultural contexts, you will be strengthening your interpersonal skills, expanding your opportunities for collaboration and professional growth, and contributing to a more inclusive, innovative, and harmonious work environment.

Cultural adaptability not only enriches your professional experience but also promotes diversity, equality, and mutual respect in the workplace, creating a space where differences are celebrated and individual potentialities are recognized and valued. By taking responsibility for developing cultural adaptability, you will be preparing yourself to meet the challenges and opportunities of an increasingly interconnected and diverse world and building the foundations for a successful and rewarding career in a global and multicultural context.

6.22 Openness to continuous learning.

Being willing to acquire new knowledge, skills, and experiences throughout your career is key to ensuring professional growth and adaptation to the demands of the ever-changing job market. Openness to continuous learning implies always being on the lookout for development opportunities, getting out of your comfort zone and committing to constant improvement and innovation.

Continuous learning throughout your career is essential to staying up-to-date, competitive, and relevant in the job market. With the rapid technological, economic and social changes taking place today, it is essential to be open to acquiring new knowledge and skills and adapting to new market requirements and trends.

Openness to continuous learning involves a willingness to explore new areas of knowledge, participate in courses, workshops, and training, and seek opportunities for personal and professional development. This requires an attitude of curiosity, thirst for knowledge, and humility to recognize that there is always something new to learn and improve.

In addition, being open to continuous learning also implies getting out of your comfort zone and facing challenges that stimulate professional growth and evolution. This may involve taking on new responsibilities, working on challenging projects, or even changing areas of expertise, seeking experiences that broaden your vision, skills, and competencies.

Committing to constant improvement and innovation is a fundamental attitude to stand out in the job market and achieve professional success. This involves a willingness to question the status quo, seek creative and innovative solutions to everyday challenges, and always be on the lookout for ways to improve your performance and add value to your work and career.

By taking responsibility for being open to continuous learning, you will invest in your personal and professional development, expanding your skills and skills, and preparing yourself to face the challenges and opportunities of the world of work with confidence and determination. Openness to continuous learning is an essential posture to ensure employability and professional growth in an increasingly dynamic, competitive and demanding work environment.

Remember that continuous learning is not only limited to acquiring new theoretical knowledge, but also involves the practical application of this knowledge, living challenging experiences, and reflecting on the learnings gained along the way.

By adopting a stance of openness to continuous learning, you will build the foundation for a solid, rewarding and ever-evolving career where personal and professional learning and growth are valued and encouraged.

6.23   Empatia digital.

In a world where interactions are increasingly digital and remote, digital empathy is a crucial skill for relating, communicating, and collaborating effectively in online environments. Digital empathy involves the ability to understand the needs, emotions, and perspectives of others even from a distance, adapt to different forms of digital communication, and maintain authentic and productive connections in virtual work environments.

In a digital context, it is essential to cultivate empathy to understand the emotions and needs of the people behind the screens, recognize the limitations and challenges of online communication, and adapt sensitively and receptively to different forms of virtual interaction. This requires a posture of active listening, genuine interest in the other, and a willingness to put oneself in the other's shoes, even without being physically present.

Digital empathy also involves the ability to adapt to different forms of online communication by understanding the nuances of digital language, emojis, abbreviations, and communication tools across different platforms. It is important to have the sensitivity to interpret the tone and intentions behind digital messages, and to seek to clarify possible misunderstandings or conflicts in a constructive and empathetic way.

Maintaining authentic and productive connections in virtual work environments requires a conscious effort to build strong, collaborative relationships based on trust, transparency, and mutual respect. This involves practicing empathy in all online interactions, acknowledging the humanity and emotions behind screens, and cultivating an inclusive, welcoming, and collaborative virtual work environment.

Taking responsibility for developing and enhancing digital empathy is critical to success and well-being in increasingly digital and remote work environments. By investing in the development of this competency, you will strengthen your communication, interpersonal and collaboration skills, and promote a work environment

6.24 Emotional resilience.

Absolutely! Emotional resilience is an essential skill for dealing with pressure, stress, and adversity in a healthy and constructive way in the workplace. It involves the ability to adapt, overcome obstacles, and learn from challenging experiences, turning them into opportunities for growth and learning.

When taking responsibility for your professional life, it's critical to develop and hone emotional resilience, along with other key soft skills such as emotional intelligence, communication skills, and teamwork. These competencies are essential to deal with the demands of the corporate world and to ensure career success and growth.

Figure 39 – Emotional resilience.

Developing emotional resilience means strengthening your ability to cope with the pressures of work, manage stress in a healthy way, and find creative and effective solutions to the challenges that arise in everyday life. This involves cultivating a positive attitude, maintaining emotional balance, seeking support when needed, and learning to adapt to change and adversity with flexibility and determination.

In addition, it is important to recognize diversity as a factor of enrichment and innovation in the workplace. Valuing the different perspectives, experiences, and skills of colleagues is essential for fostering an inclusive, collaborative, and creative work environment where diversity is seen as an asset and a source of learning and growth for all.

By investing in the development of emotional resilience and other important soft skills, you will prepare yourself to face the challenges and opportunities of professional life with confidence, assertiveness, and serenity. Emotional resilience not only contributes to your own well-being and professional success, but also to strengthening interpersonal relationships, promoting a healthy organizational climate, and building more efficient and resilient teams.

Taking responsibility for your professional life involves a commitment to continuously develop and enhance your skills and competencies, including emotional resilience, to face the challenges and changes of the job market with determination and effectiveness. By investing in your personal and professional development, you will build the foundations for a solid, rewarding and constantly evolving career, where the ability to adapt, grow and overcome adversity becomes a differential and a springboard for success and professional fulfillment.

By cultivating the skills of self-management, proactivity, resilience, effective communication, critical thinking, empathy, leadership, honesty, problem-solving, adaptability, collaboration, among others, you will be strengthening your ability to deal with challenges, achieve your goals and stand out in the job market.

Taking responsibility for your professional life requires a constant commitment to personal and professional development, honing the soft skills needed to meet the challenges of the ever-changing work environment, build healthy and productive relationships, and achieve professional success in a sustainable and meaningful way.

By integrating these soft skills into your routine and professional practice, you will not only be expanding your individual capabilities, but also contributing to building a more collaborative, diverse, and inclusive work environment, where everyone's personal and professional growth is valued and encouraged. Taking responsibility for your professional life is a key step in achieving your goals and realizing your full potential in the business world and beyond.

"Burnout is the feeling of being stuck in a job that doesn't fulfill us, of wasting years of life doing something that has no meaning to us."

Arianna Huffington[4]

---

[4] Arianna Huffington is a Greek-American writer, journalist, businesswoman, and columnist. She is the co-founder and former editor-in-chief of The Huffington Post, one of the largest news and blogging sites in the world.

7 BURNOUT OF PROFESSIONALS.

> *"What good is the money, if you don't have the health to enjoy it?"*
>
> Writer Thais Coutinho

Burnout is a relevant and worrisome topic in the context of mental health and well-being of professionals, being widely studied and debated by researchers and health professionals.

In this text, I will address burnout from a medical perspective, citing some renowned authors and their contributions to the understanding of this phenomenon.

Maslow (1972) describes burnout as a state of emotional, physical, and mental exhaustion that results from a chronically stressful and exhausting work environment. According to the author, burnout is characterized by symptoms such as extreme fatigue, lack of motivation, and difficulty concentrating, negatively affecting the individual's professional performance and quality of life.

Psychiatrist Freudenberger (1974) was one of the first scholars to investigate burnout in a more systematic way, highlighting the importance of psychological and emotional factors in its manifestation.

For him, burnout is closely linked to emotional exhaustion and the feeling of disillusionment in relation to work, manifesting itself as a gradual process of exhaustion of the individual's physical and mental energies.

Figure 40 - Herbert J. Freudenberger.

Psychiatrist Maslach (1982), in turn, developed one of the most widely used assessment scales to measure burnout, known as the Maslach Burnout Inventory (MBI).

Maslach identifies burnout as a complex phenomenon, resulting from the interaction between work demands, available social support, and the subject's personal characteristics, which directly impact their ability to deal with the stress and pressures of the work environment.

In a recent study, Shirom and Melamed (2006) investigated the relationship between burnout and workers' physical health, highlighting the adverse effects of burnout on cardiovascular health, the immune system, and the incidence of chronic diseases.

For the authors, burnout is not only restricted to the aspect and psychological, but also directly affects the physical health of individuals, increasing the risk of diseases and health problems associated with chronic stress.

Figure 41 - ChristinaMaslach.

In another study, Schaufeli and Peeters (2000) proposed a widely accepted theoretical model to explain burnout, known as the attrition model. According to the authors, burnout is the result of an imbalance between the demands of work and the resources available to deal with these demands, leading to emotional exhaustion, depersonalization, and decreased personal fulfillment.

It is important to note that burnout not only affects healthcare professionals, but also workers in several other areas, such as education, services, and technology.

Appendix A. Maslach Burnout Inventory (MBI)

The Maslach Burnout Inventory (MBI) is the most commonly used tool to assess the risk of burnout which was developed by Christina Maslach (1981). The validity and reliability study of this inventory made by Ergin (1993) in Turkey.

Maslach C, Jackson SE. The measurement of experienced burnout. J Organ Behav.. 1981;2:99–113.

Ergin C. Adaptation and Validity of MBI for Measuring Burnout Among Turkish Physicians and Nurses, 7th National Psychology Congress, Bayraktar R (ed.), Turkish Psychologists Association, Ankara D 1, 1993, 143–154. (in Turkish).

Maslach Burnout Inventory (MBI)

The inventory consists of 22 questions which have five graded Likert-type answers. To determine the risk of burnout, the MBI explores three sub-scales: emotional exhaustion, depersonalization and personal accomplishment.

A high score in the first and third sections and a low score in the second section may indicate burnout.

Questions	Never	Rarely	Sometimes	Frequently	Always
I. Emotional Exhaustion					
I feel emotionally drained from my work	0	1	2	3	4
I feel used up at the end of the workday	0	1	2	3	4
I feel fatigued when I get up in the morning and have to face another day on the job	0	1	2	3	4
Working with people all day is really a strain for me	0	1	2	3	4
I feel burned out from my work	0	1	2	3	4
I feel frustrated by my job	0	1	2	3	4
I feel I'm working too hard on my job	0	1	2	3	4
Working with people directly puts too much stress on me	0	1	2	3	4
I feel like I'm at the end of my rope	0	1	2	3	4
II. Personal Accomplishment					
I can easily understand how my recipients feel about things	0	1	2	3	4
I deal very effectively with the problems of my recipients	0	1	2	3	4
I feel I'm positively influencing other people's lives through my work	0	1	2	3	4
I feel very energetic	0	1	2	3	4
I can easily create a relaxed atmosphere with my recipients	0	1	2	3	4
I feel exhilarated after working closely with my recipients	0	1	2	3	4
I have accomplished many worthwhile things in this job	0	1	2	3	4
In my work, I deal with emotional problems very calmly	0	1	2	3	4
III. Depersonalization					
I feel I treat some recipients as if they were impersonal 'objects'	0	1	2	3	4
I've become more callous toward people since I took this job	0	1	2	3	4
I worry that this job is hardening me emotionally	0	1	2	3	4
I don't really care what happens to some recipients	0	1	2	3	4
I feel recipients blame me for some of their problems	0	1	2	3	4

Figure 42 - Maslach Burnout Inventory.

However, due to the demanding and stressful nature of many healthcare professions, medical professionals, nurses, and other healthcare workers are particularly susceptible to burnout and its negative consequences for health and well-being.

Given this scenario, it is essential that managers, leaders, and health professionals are aware of the signs of burnout and adopt preventive and supportive measures to promote a healthy and balanced work environment. Implementing self-care strategies, establishing clear boundaries between personal and professional life, and providing emotional and psychological support to healthcare professionals are key to preventing and coping with burnout effectively.

Burnout is thus a multifaceted and complex phenomenon that affects millions of workers around the world, including healthcare professionals. Through the contributions and studies of renowned authors in the medical field, it is possible to better understand the causes, symptoms and consequences of burnout, and to adopt effective measures to promote the well-being and mental health of professionals, thus ensuring a better quality of life in the workplace and in society as a whole.

We're all familiar with the risks of burnout. The consequences are dire and include.

- Job dissatisfaction.
- Depression.
- Inefficient decision-making.
- Lack of autonomy, engagement, motivation and passion.
- Problems from health-related issues such as depression, heart disease, and even death.

Some evidence suggests that entrepreneurs are more at risk of burnout because they tend to be extremely passionate about their work and more socially isolated, have limited safety nets, and operate with high uncertainty.

Are you a business owner and worried that you might fall victim to burnout? You're not alone. Recent studies reveal that a quarter of busy entrepreneurs experience moderate degrees of burnout at some point in their careers.

It's no secret that running a business. or even your career, exposes you to stressful situations. The key is to learn how to deal with stressors in healthy ways.

You need to learn how to keep your motivation levels high, your stress levels low, and avoid burnout when leading a company.

Suppose you are about to open a new business or a promising franchise opportunity. In this case, you need to pay attention to how much you personally invest and how much stress you are subjected to.

Are you burning the candle at both ends?

Do you act like you're a machine that can keep going no matter what?

Even the strongest individuals who are passionate about entrepreneurship can't keep up that pace or work under constant stress without eventually becoming a victim of their effort.

Another potential cause for burnout is feeling like your hands are tied. Is there resistance in your business that deflates your motivation around many important decisions? Do you experience decision fatigue? If so, then it's likely that stress and, consequently, burnout are waiting for you around the corner.

Low mental health maintenance is a significant factor when it comes to burnout. You'll feel drained of energy if you think too much or worry too often. This leads to feeling overwhelmed and like you no longer have control over the business.

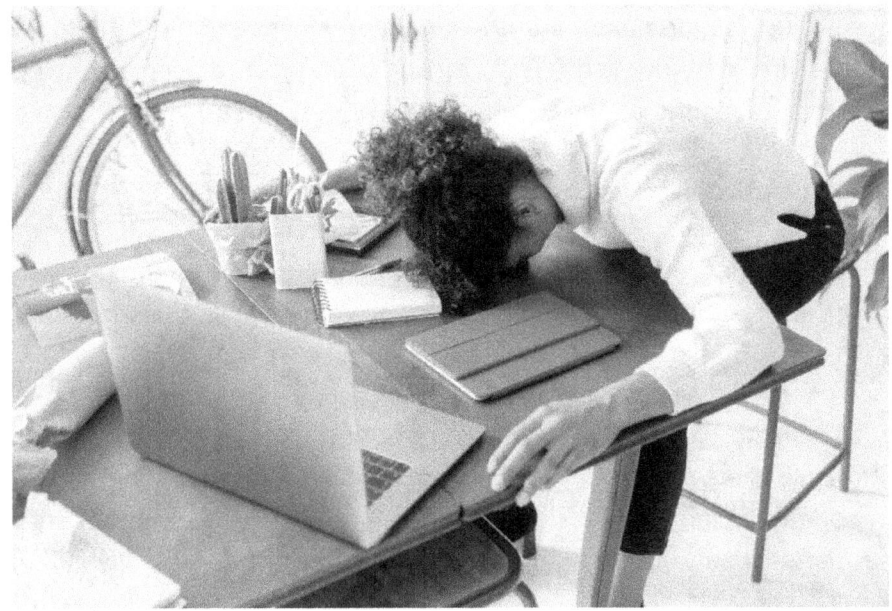

Figure 43 –Burnout.

Every entrepreneur plays a variety of roles early in their career, especially if they are building a business from scratch for the first time.

To achieve balance while pursuing goals, it is essential for entrepreneurs to define their values and create clear boundaries in the workplace. Managing anxiety before it spirals out of control is crucial to focusing your energy on business success.

Before building any business model, you should define what your company does in the simplest terms possible. You should do the same in your own life as an entrepreneur. Define your values at the beginning, both in your business and in your personal life.

You can't do everything, and it's important to understand that when you start your journey. Work with a business strategy expert to set clear business goals, determine the focus of your business, and identify places where you need to build or expand your team.

With these values defined and addressed in your business, you should take care of your personal life. Whether you're just starting out or you've been an entrepreneur for many years, take time to define what you will and won't do for your company.

7.1 How far will you go to achieve and sustain success?

What things in your life are worth sacrificing for the entrepreneurial journey, and what things are too important to sacrifice? Answering these questions will reveal your value system and allow you to narrow your focus.

It's easy to want to please customers or your boss by doing everything, but that's not sustainable. You can build a brand reputation—and a personal reputation—without compromising boundaries. Interact with your customers strategically, making sure they know you'll give them what you promised.

At the same time, it's important to set boundaries at work, especially if you offer a service that requires you to interact with the same customers over and over again.

Set personal boundaries around communication first. Limit your work hours to traditional work schedules, or a more rigorous 8-hour daily schedule, and train yourself to respect the line between personal and professional.

This may mean that customers can't get access to you right away, but it's essential to adhere to this limit if you want to avoid burnout. You can also set boundaries with customers, letting them know in advance when you're available or what forms of communication are appropriate (email, text, phone call).

Clients will respect that you have a life outside of work, especially if you clearly communicate your own expectations around the relationship you have with them.

Having work hours and personal hours is also a good way to train your mind to zero in on the present. When you're working, you can focus on your clients and your business, knowing that you can handle personal matters later. When you're relaxing after a long day with clients, you can really relax without annoying work issues clouding your mind.

Figure 44 "It may be a slow burn, but at the limit we have a real explosion.

It's important to build these boundaries into your strategy ahead of time so that you have them in place when you need them. It's much harder to implement a new boundary with a needy customer that's been around for a long time than it is to set boundaries with a new client.

Every entrepreneur experiences the push needed at the beginning of a business. Building your own company requires so much of your mental space that it can feel like your whole life. That's not wrong, but it's not sustainable either. If you want to be in business for the long haul, you need to plan.

The key to a lifelong career in entrepreneurship is to create boundaries built around your value system and apply them from the start.

If you spend more than a few years walking along the "be your own boss" route that is entrepreneurship, you're bound to experience burnout and discouragement at one time or another.

Burnout can occur when you're deep into developing flaw-infested products before making a single sale, or it can occur when you're in the midst of operating a well-oiled sales-generating machine.

Employing some not-so-obvious coping strategies can help you overcome entrepreneurial fatigue and reinvigorate your passion for running and growing your business.

7.2   Symptoms of burnout.

If any of the symptoms below sound eerily familiar, you may also be experiencing entrepreneurial burnout.

Figure 45 – It's amazing how you don't notice the symptoms of burnout!

7.2.1 Do co-workers become your enemies?

Any non-entrepreneur can assume that their employers love and appreciate their work, as they are the ones who are keeping the business afloat.

While this is true most of the time, professionals who run high-volume or high-level customer interaction deals can get burned out with people very quickly.

When professionals find themselves in the field with hundreds of inbound inquiries or endless customer support requests, it can all be too much.

If you're a professional who suddenly can't stand your tasks, you may be a victim of people-oriented burnout. There are a few solutions to deal with.

1. Employ an email forwarding chatbot or autoresponders to inbound email inquiries, setting a reasonable expectation around response times. Just because you run a business doesn't mean you have to be accessible 24/7 or respond to potential customers within two hours. Set clear expectations around the response time that works for you and your team – whether it's three hours or three business days. That way, you won't feel like every incoming request requires immediate action.
2. Outsource customer service completely. There are great and affordable customer support options, from live chatbots to answering services to virtual assistants, that can get most inbound inquiries out your doorstep.
3. Batch your customer-facing tasks and focus them on one or two days a week. If you choose to respond on Mondays and Thursdays, customers will never have to wait more than three days for a response, but you will have five quiet, peaceful, people-free days per week. It's a win-win for sure!

7.2.2 Do you have Monday panic?

One of the advantages of running your own business is the ability to set your preferred hours and work as many days and hours as you want.

Somewhere along the way, you can develop a more conventional workweek with a "Monday" of its own, or the day that marks the dreaded start of a grueling week.

If you find yourself dreading Mondays, or any day you consider your weekend's funeral, you may want to shake things up and rebuild your schedule.

Kick the "conventional" workweek and throw a weekend or two in between your workdays. Changing your schedule can renew your inspiration and resurrect the freedom that drew you to the entrepreneurial lifestyle in the first place.

7.2.3   Is your life a life sentence without parole?

Freedom may have drawn you into the entrepreneurial lifestyle, but once your business begins to consume your thoughts 24/7/365, even in your sleep, you may be chained to a prison of your own making.

If you can't remember the last time you took a vacation and the thought of leaving emails unread for a day gives you goosebumps, it may be time for a decontamination with a major disconnect from work and life online.

If your business won't grant you parole, you'll have to fake your own escape. Lucky for you, this can be done simply through automation.

7.2.4   Are shiny new opportunities always catching your eye?

Sometimes too much good stuff can be a problem, even if that thing is your business. Contrary to popular belief, it is possible to run multiple successful trades at the same time.

If you find yourself drawn toward a new business opportunity or financial upheaval, don't dismiss it as an unnecessary distraction or a waste of time right away. Instead, analyze why you're attracted to this new opportunity.

Experiencing the entrepreneurial itch to embark on a new project may not be a bad thing at all and some of us are natural creators who will always want something new on our plate.

Utilizing several completely different skills can keep you engaged, inspired, and excited about each independent project, while also honing diverse skills that can complement each other.

> *You might be surprised at the synergies that come from their seemingly different projects.*

But it is essential to filter which opportunity you are going to allocate your energies to and not succumb to every new chance to undertake.

7.2.5   Is LinkedIn the terror of your existence?

You open LinkedIn, click on "notifications," and instantly realize what a mistake it was, as you're bombarded with an endless stream of positive updates and congratulatory milestones from your network.

It seems like everyone raised yet another $10 million seed funding round, reached their $100K crowdfunding goal, ran a promotion on their 9-5, or was featured in the news for their company's new product launch.

Most of us think of LinkedIn as a "professional" social network, one that seems to bypass the "fakeness" and "stand out the reel" of flashier and openly self-centered platforms like Instagram.

But the truth is, LinkedIn is also social media, and user psychology doesn't change drastically just because you consider something a "professional" platform. People post their highs and keep their lows to themselves.

The problem is that on LinkedIn, you're there to be judged professionally on your career or business progress, so the reputational repercussions of a lesser post can seem much more severe for your future jobs and gain power.

Once you realize that LinkedIn is just an IG for people who would rather brag about their work or their business than their oversaturated selfie, you can take those notifications with a dozen grains of salt and a pinch of pepper.

If LinkedIn is becoming more discouraging than encouraging, you may want to take a temporary break. Your business probably won't fall apart if you leave LinkedIn for a few weeks unless you make the majority of your sales on LinkedIn, in which case you may want to avoid notifications and keep your focus on ads and responding to customer messages.

There are probably a million other higher ROI activities[5] you could devote your time to than drooling over the updates of your network's LinkedIn idlers and envy-inducers.

Most of the real work happens behind closed doors and outside of LinkedIn anyway. Social media is just a place to share the "before and after," but they rarely explain the journey in between.

7.3   These clues can prevent burnout from setting in.

We often see burnout as an inevitable side effect of too much work, too little relaxation, or the reaction to a relentless and depressing sequence of results. When

---

[5] Acronym for Return on Investment, or Return on Investment, in Portuguese. In a simpler way, it is the relationship between what was invested and the profit in marketing actions and campaigns.

you put it that way, burnout sounds like a terrible culmination of negativity and something to be avoided at all costs.

I do not agree with that assessment. Of course, a steady stream of losses can discourage a person or rob them of their motivation. However, burnout can happen even when sales are at a record high.

Remember the case of multi-Olympic champion Simone Biles who withdrew from the competition during the trials?

The five symptoms of burnout presented in the previous section provide a valuable opportunity to reassess root causes and make positive changes to alter and improve your business, alter priorities, and increase focus on a reduced number of operations to ensure you are making the most of your entrepreneurial skill sets, ambition, and inspiration.

What good is a profitable business if we can't handle the journey to build it or to handle the day-to-day operations that keep it running?

Recognizing your potential for burnout can give rise to an unexpected new opportunity to manage your ventures, reduce your stress level, and at the same time completely expand your entrepreneurial journey.

There are only two kinds of people who can say that it is impossible to change the world. those who are afraid to try and those who are afraid of your success.

Ray Goforth.

8 SUICIDE FOR PROFESSIONAL REASONS.

Suicide as a tragic outcome of professional problems is a complex phenomenon that has been gaining more attention within the field of mental health.

For a long time, psychiatry treated suicide as a phenomenon intrinsically linked to mental disorders and psychological imbalances, looking less at the social and environmental factors that can also play significant roles. However, in the last decade, a greater understanding of the role occupational stress plays in mental health has reshaped this view.

Work-related suicide can be understood as the culmination of an identity crisis and a sense of worthlessness, precipitated by abusive work environments, unattainable performance expectations, and a culture of silence around personal vulnerability.

Suicide, in this context, arises not only from individual mental disorders, but also from a collective failure to create work environments that value psychological well-being. Excessive pressures for results, fear of unemployment, and lack of support can lead to a state of despair where the individual feels they have lost control of their lives and see no other way out than suicide.

This perspective is echoed by other scholars in the field, such as psychiatrists Allison Miller, Mathew J. Spittal, Jane Pirkis, and Anthony D LaMontagne and recorded in their book Suicide by occupation: systematic review and meta-analysis (2013) who emphasize that the association between professional burnout and suicidal ideation cannot be ignored.

The increasingly insistent demands for efficiency and professional success can be emotionally draining and ultimately unsustainable, leading to inevitable emotional burnout when there is no adequate support.

The stigma previously associated with discussing suicide and mental health in the workplace has been decreasing, and there is now a growing recognition that organizations have a responsibility to care for the mental health of their employees.

Employee assistance programs, stress management training, and more flexible work policies are some of the steps being taken to confront this issue.

Figure 46 – Alison Miller, Matthew J. Spital, Jane Pirkis at Anthony de Lamontagne

In addition, it is essential to emphasize that the preventive approach to suicide requires a multifaceted strategy. Prevention should involve not only support in the workplace, but also access to quality mental health care, community support, and the promotion of open dialogue about mental health issues. To paraphrase Karsten Michael, the sense of belonging and being valued is a vital antidote to the existential crisis that can lead to suicide.

Attention to warning signs, such as changes in behavior, decline in job performance, social isolation, and verbalizations about hopelessness, is critical. It is necessary to encourage a culture where asking for help is seen as a sign of strength, not weakness.

Work-related suicide is a complex phenomenon that has received more attention in recent years due to increased pressures in the workplace and increased awareness of mental health. There are a number of factors that can lead a person to consider suicide due to work-related issues, and it is important to address these issues holistically and preventively.

8.1   Factors for a suicide for professional reasons.

One of the reasons for suicide for professional reasons is chronic stress in the workplace. Excessive pressures related to performance goals, tight deadlines, fierce competition, and task overload can lead to a state of emotional and physical exhaustion, known as burnout. Burnout is a significant risk factor for suicide, as it can lead to feelings of hopelessness, lack of purpose, and social isolation.

In addition to burnout, workplace bullying and toxicity are also common reasons for suicide for professional reasons. Bullying, discrimination, sexual harassment, and psychological violence are all forms of abuse that can have a devastating impact on an individual's mental health.

Feelings of helplessness, humiliation, and devaluation can lead to a deep sense of despair and alienation, making suicide an attempt to escape emotional pain.

Another factor that contributes to work-related suicide is a lack of support and resources to address mental health issues in the workplace. Many organizations still have cultures that discourage the expression of emotional vulnerabilities and fragilities, creating an environment where employees feel isolated and unsupported to deal with their struggles. Lack of access to mental health services, such as therapy and counseling, can also be a significant obstacle for those who are struggling with emotional issues.

Additionally, the culture of success and productivity at any cost can contribute to the internal pressure individuals feel to achieve unrealistic standards of professional performance and success. The constant comparison with peers, the pursuit of perfection, and the feeling of never being good enough can lead to a cycle of unsustainable self-demand, leading to emotional exhaustion and psychological burnout.

Economic instability and job insecurity can also be reasons for suicide for professional reasons. Fear of unemployment, precarious job market, and uncertainty regarding the financial future can aggravate feelings of despair and helplessness, leading individuals to consider suicide as a way out of their problems.

Faced with this complex scenario, it is essential to adopt a preventive and integrated approach to addressing suicide for professional reasons. Organizations should foster healthy work environments that value employee well-being and encourage open communication about mental health issues. Suicide prevention programs, mental health training, and easy access to support resources are essential for creating more welcoming and supportive organizational cultures.

8.2   Suicide due to job loss.

Job loss is an event that can have a profound impact on an individual's self-esteem and self-confidence. Work is often more than just a source of income, it is also a central element in building personal identity and a sense of self-worth.

Thus, when dismissal occurs, it is as if part of the individual's emotional structures are shaken. The feeling of no longer being useful, competent, or valued can generate a real earthquake in the person's self-image, leading them to a cycle of negative self-criticism that can result in self-destructive thoughts.

Self-esteem and self-confidence are critical to a person's psychological and emotional well-being, and job loss can undermine these foundations significantly. The sense of failure and inadequacy that often accompanies quitting can lead to a downward spiral of negative thoughts about oneself, fueling a cycle of self-devaluation and hopelessness.

The perception that one is no longer able to contribute meaningfully or be recognized for one's abilities can erode an individual's self-esteem, making room for feelings of worthlessness and helplessness.

Additionally, the link between work, identity, and self-worth can make job loss an especially painful blow for many people. The notion of belonging to a group, the achievement of a purpose, and external validation through work can be essential pillars in building self-image and maintaining emotional balance.

When these pillars are shaken by resignation, the person may feel lost, disoriented, and aimless, profoundly impacting their self-confidence and their ability to see themselves in a positive light.

The cycle of negative self-criticism triggered by job loss can become a mental trap that is difficult to escape. The inner voice that echoes feelings of failure, incompetence, and the feeling of no longer being useful, competent, or valued can become a constant reminder of the individual's supposed flaws and flaws, leading to a progressive deterioration of self-image and self-esteem.

In this context, the mind tends to focus only on its own weaknesses, ignoring past achievements and present virtues. This cycle of self-deprecation can generate a state of deep despondency and hopelessness, opening the door to self-destructive thoughts and even the consideration of suicide as a way to relieve emotional pain and psychological distress.

Job loss is not just a professional setback, but has the potential to profoundly shake an individual's emotional and mental structures, significantly impacting their mental health and emotional well-being. It is crucial to recognize the complexity and severity of these challenges, seeking emotional support strategies, psychological counseling, and support networks that can help the individual cope in a healthy and constructive way with the emotional repercussions of job loss.

Fostering an environment of understanding, acceptance, and solidarity is essential to prevent devastating consequences and provide the necessary support for those who face these kinds of challenges in their lives. It is important to emphasize that suicide is a complex and multifaceted problem, and that prevention requires a joint effort from the whole society.

By addressing issues related to suicide for professional reasons in a compassionate and proactive way, we can help reduce stigma around mental health, promote healthier work environments, and save lives. Mental health should be a priority in all spheres of society, and suicide for professional reasons is a problem that can no longer be ignored.

When a person is laid off, they may experience an intense sense of failure and helplessness. Job loss can be perceived as a personal rejection, a failure to meet one's own and societal expectations, and a threat to financial security and stability. The feeling of helplessness in the face of the situation and uncertainty about the future can generate a state of deep sadness and despair, which can lead to suicidal thoughts.

Lack of emotional and social support during this difficult time can also contribute to suicide risk. Shame, social isolation, and fear of being judged by others can prevent a person from seeking help and support, increasing feelings of loneliness and helplessness. The absence of an effective support network and resources to cope with the stress and anxiety related to job loss can exacerbate the situation and amplify feelings of hopelessness and helplessness.

In addition, the financial pressure that comes with losing one's job is also a factor that can lead to suicide. Lack of income, accumulating debt, and worrying about providing for one's family can generate an unbearable level of stress and anxiety, leading to a feeling of hopelessness and helplessness.

The lack of prospects for re-employment and the feeling of being trapped in a cycle of financial hardship can seem like an insurmountable barrier for many people, leading them to consider suicide as a way to escape the situation.

It is important to emphasize that suicide due to job loss is not a rational decision, but rather a tragic outcome of a set of emotional, psychological, and social factors. The internal struggle that leads a person to consider suicide is an extreme manifestation of psychological distress and a cry for help for help. Therefore, it is critical to approach this issue with empathy, compassion, and understanding, providing emotional support, psychological treatment, and resources to effectively address the challenges arising from job loss.

Preventing suicide from job loss requires a multifaceted approach that involves not only the affected individual, but also family, friends, co-workers, institutions, and society as a whole.

The creation of emotional support networks, the encouragement of seeking professional help, the implementation of programs to promote mental health in the workplace, the availability of financial guidance resources, and awareness of the importance of open communication about mental health issues are some of the measures that can be adopted to prevent suicide due to job loss.

It is also essential to combat the stigma around mental health and suicide by fostering an open and welcoming dialogue about these issues. Public education about the warning signs of suicidal behavior, the importance of seeking professional help, and the resources available for emotional support are key to raising awareness and reducing the stigma associated with suicide.

Finally, the prevention of suicide due to job loss requires a collective and supportive approach that recognizes the complexity and seriousness of the issues involved.

By fostering healthy work environments, encouraging the expression of vulnerabilities, providing emotional support, and ensuring access to mental health resources, we can help protect people's lives and emotional health in times of crisis. Caring, compassion, and empathy are essential tools in preventing suicide and building a healthier, more welcoming society for all.

Suicidology in the professional context offers a revealing microcosm of systemic failures in mental health care. Psychiatry professionals, as well as managers and co-workers, are called to recognize the seriousness and complex reality of suicide, intervening in a proactive and humanized way to preserve lives and promote mental health in the professional environment.

8.3 KAROSHI.

Karoshi is a Japanese term meaning "death by overwork" or "death by overwork." It is a phenomenon that has become increasingly relevant in several countries around the world, but it first gained prominence in Japan, where overwork is a deep-rooted cultural issue.

Karoshi occurs when an individual is pushed to the limit physically, mentally, and emotionally as a result of long working hours, intense pressure, lack of adequate rest, and chronic job-related stress. This condition can lead to a range of physical and mental health problems, including heart disease, sleep disorders, depression, anxiety, and even suicide.

In Japan, where the culture of hard work and extreme commitment to the company is widespread, karoshi has become a national concern.

The country is known for having one of the highest working hours in the world, with many workers working constant overtime, often late into the night and on weekends. This pattern of overwork has been linked to a significant increase in karoshi cases, with workers suffering the physical and psychological consequences of overwork.

Figure 47 - Vítima do Karoshi.

Symptoms of karoshi can include chronic fatigue, insomnia, anxiety, depression, irritability, trouble concentrating, physical pain, increased risk of cardiovascular disease, and stress-related illnesses.

Chronic stress associated with overwork can compromise the mental and emotional health of workers, leading to severe exhaustion, discouragement, and even the development of more serious psychological disorders.

In addition to the individual impacts on workers' health, karoshi also has social and economic repercussions. The high incidence of deaths related to excessive work can result in high costs for health systems, productivity losses in companies, and a negative organizational climate in the workplace.

The fear of losing one's job, the pressure for better and better results, and the vicious cycle of exacerbated competitiveness can all contribute to a toxic and unhealthy work environment, increasing the risk of karoshi and negatively impacting the quality of life of workers.

Importantly, karoshi is not just an individual problem, but a reflection of broader structural issues related to work practices, organizational culture, and social values around employment and professional success. The need to promote a healthy work, life, and emotional well-being balance for workers is essential to prevent karoshi and ensure healthier and more sustainable work environments.

To combat karoshi, it is necessary to implement measures that promote the health and well-being of workers, such as limiting overtime, promoting flexible policies in working hours, encouraging the use of vacations and rest periods, raising awareness of the importance of mental health, and creating safe spaces for workers to express their difficulties and seek help when necessary.

In addition, it is essential that companies and government authorities take responsibility for promoting a healthy organizational culture that values work-life balance, open and transparent communication, care for the mental health of employees, and respect for each worker's individual limits.

Implementing workplace wellness policies, stress and anxiety prevention programs, and fostering a collaborative and supportive work environment are important steps in preventing karoshi and protecting the health and well-being of workers.

Karoshi is a Japanese term that means "death by overwork."

It is a phenomenon that has gained prominence due to the increasing incidence of cases in which individuals suffer fatal consequences as a result of strenuous work-related workloads, excessive pressure, and chronic stress.

In Japan, a country known for its intense work culture and long office hours, karoshi has become a national concern. Many Japanese workers face grueling hours, often working overtime and giving up adequate rest for the sake of work. This mindset of extreme dedication to the company has led to a significant increase in karoshi cases, with workers suffering the physical and mental consequences of overwork.

In addition to individual impacts, karoshi also has social and economic repercussions. High rates of overwork-related deaths result in substantial costs to health systems, productivity losses in companies, and a stressful work environment, undermining workers' quality of life and the overall health of society.

Normosis is wrongly indoctrinating many men and women who could, if they wanted to, be much more authentic and happy.

Martha Medeiros[6]

---

[6] Brazilian writer and journalist known for her chronicles and poems.

9   A NORMOSE.

Professional normosis is a contemporary phenomenon that refers to the internalization of behavior patterns, beliefs, and values considered "normal" by society, but which can be harmful to the health and well-being of workers.

These patterns are often associated with a culture of hyperproductivity, excessive competition, chronic stress, a lack of work-life balance, and a constant pursuit of perfection and success at any cost.

Professionals affected by normosis often adopt behaviors such as the incessant search for success, the pressure for immediate results, exacerbated self-demand, and a lack of work-life balance. Long working hours, excessive overtime, lack of time for rest and leisure, unbridled competitiveness, and the constant search for perfection are just a few examples of the characteristics of this phenomenon.

Among these behaviors are long working hours, excessive overtime, lack of time for rest and leisure, pressure for immediate results, unbridled competitiveness, and exacerbated self-demand.

The normosis of professionals is often related to a work environment that demands high performance, increasingly ambitious goals and a constant search for excellence.

In this scenario, employees are constantly pressured to live up to the expectations and standards imposed, often to the detriment of their health and well-being.

The fear of failure, the need to live up to the expectations of superiors, and the relentless pursuit of recognition and success can lead professionals to sacrifice their physical, emotional, and personal relationships in the name of work.

The culture of normosis in professionals can be fueled by several factors, such as the pressure for performance and increasingly ambitious goals, the fear of failure, the need to live up to the expectations of superiors, and the relentless search for

recognition and success. Too often, professionals find themselves in a constant cycle of stress and overwhelm, sacrificing their physical, mental, and emotional health in the name of work.

With technology facilitating constant access to work, many professionals find themselves in a continuous cycle of availability and demands, which makes it difficult to establish the moments of rest and leisure necessary to recharge their energy and maintain balanced mental health.

Figure 48- Normosis?

In addition, the lack of clear boundaries between personal and professional life contributes to the perpetuation of professional normosis. With the constant accessibility to work provided by technology, many professionals find themselves involved in a vicious cycle of availability and demands, which makes it even more difficult to disconnect and establish moments of rest and leisure essential for balance and mental health.

It is important to emphasize that the normosis of professionals not only affects individual health and well-being, but also has repercussions on organizations, reflecting in an exhausting work environment, with high levels of stress, low employee satisfaction, and a drop in productivity.

The lack of work-life balance, task overload, and constant pressure for results can generate a toxic organizational climate, harming the work climate, motivation, and employee engagement.

Figure 49 – Children's normose.

Additionally, it is essential for managers to be aware of signs of overload and stress among employees, fostering an organizational culture that encourages open dialogue, empathy, and mutual support. The promotion of flexibility in working hours, the valorization of rest time and the implementation of practices that favor the balance between personal and professional life are important steps to prevent and combat normosis in professionals.

It is necessary to recognize that the normosis of professionals is not an individual problem, but a reflection of broader structural issues related to work culture, social expectations, and the way companies organize and encourage the performance of their employees.

By promoting a healthy, balanced, and welcoming work culture, organizations can contribute to the well-being and satisfaction of employees, creating an environment conducive to the personal and professional growth of everyone involved.

Normosis and burnout are two related phenomena that have become increasingly present in the contemporary workplace. While normosis refers to the internalization of behavior patterns that are harmful to the health and well-being of professionals, burnout is a syndrome characterized by emotional exhaustion, depersonalization, and decreased professional fulfillment, resulting from chronic stress at work.

The connection between normosis and burnout is associated with excessive pressure, task overload, and the constant pursuit of performance and success, which are common features in both conditions.

Professionals affected by normosis are more susceptible to developing burnout due to the adoption of behaviors and attitudes that are harmful to mental and physical health, such as the lack of boundaries between personal and professional life, exacerbated self-demand, and the inability to disconnect from work.

Normosis can play a key role in the genesis of burnout, as the patterns of behavior associated with the internalization of social norms and expectations can lead professionals to submit to an excessive workload, constant performance pressures, and a continuous cycle of stress.

This combination of factors can result in emotional exhaustion, depersonalization, and loss of meaning at work, all of which are characteristic symptoms of burnout.

The pressure for immediate results, unbridled competitiveness, the constant search for success, and a lack of work-life balance are just some of the common elements between normosis and burnout.

Both phenomena are intrinsically linked to contemporary work culture, which often demands professionals to perform beyond their capabilities, resulting in negative consequences for their physical, mental, and emotional health.

Raising awareness about the importance of identifying early signs of normosis and burnout and the search for coping and prevention strategies are essential to ensure the health and well-being of professionals in the workplace.

In addition, the involvement and support of organizations are essential to create an environment that promotes the resilience and mental health of employees, reducing the negative impacts of normosis and burnout.

Normose, a concept originally explored by authors such as Jean-Yves Leloup, Pierre Weil, and Roberto Crema. In analyzing this concept, the authors argue that normality can be pathological when it leads to a state of conformity that prevents the individual from living authentically and healthily.

Figure 50 - Jean-Yves Leloup.

Figure 51 - Pierre Weil.

Figure 52 - Roberto Crema.

Considering the thoughts of these authors, it is possible to highlight some central points of the discussion on normosis:

1. Social Compliance. Normosis arises from the pressure to conform to societal expectations. What is considered "normal" is often shaped by social, cultural, and religious institutions, and deviation from these norms can be seen as pathological or undesirable.
2. Authenticity. The concept of normosis questions the idea that adhering to social norms equates to a healthy way of life. On the contrary, it suggests that authenticity and critical questioning of norms may be more conducive to mental health than conformity.
3. Health and Disease. Thinking about normosis sheds light on how definitions of health and disease are constructed. Rather than viewing "abnormality" as a disease, the authors propose that thoughtless adherence to normality may be more harmful.
4. Personal development. Normosis theorists argue that personal growth and development depend on the individual's ability to transcend the limits

imposed by the oppressing normality. The pathology of normality lies in the inhibition of personal expression and stagnation.

5. Social Criticism. Normosis is also a social critique that proposes a reflection on how established values and practices can perpetuate inequalities and injustices, suggesting that systematic changes are necessary to promote a healthier and more psychologically liberating society.
6. Individuality versus Collectivity. Normosis highlights the conflict between individuality and collective standards. The authors suggest that while society imposes norms to maintain order and predictability, it is essential for the individual to maintain a sense of personal identity and purpose that may at times be at odds with those norms.
7. Reflection and Awareness. Combating the concept of normosis, the authors defend the importance of continuous reflection and the development of consciousness. They suggest that an examined life is less susceptible to the harmful effects of normosis and promotes psychological well-being and genuine happiness.
8. Holistic Wellness. Viewing normosis as a barrier to well-being, the authors' narrative promotes a holistic view of health that integrates physical, mental, emotional, and spiritual aspects. They are thus opposed to reductionist views that limit the understanding of human health to a purely physical or biological state.

The idea of normosis invites a critical reassessment of social norms and the search for a balance between social adaptation and the preservation of the authentic self. The authors of this concept demand a greater appreciation of the diversity of experiences and perspectives, arguing that true health emerges at the intersection between the unique being and the community in which it is inserted.

This balance is seen as the key to a more fulfilled life and less susceptible to the problems that come from conformism and pathological "normality."

"When an employee resigns, most of the time they're not quitting the company, they're quitting their boss."

Alexander Den Heijer[7]

---

[7] American author who has become known for several quotes in the field of motivation and personal development.

10 PROFESSIONAL EXPECTATIONS AND FRUSTRATIONS.

Reflecting on professional expectations and frustrations is key to understanding the impact that the work environment can have on people's lives. Often, the expectations created around one's career and professional success can be a source of motivation, but also of anguish and disappointment. To illustrate this complexity, I resort to some quotes from renowned authors who address this theme.

To begin with, it is important to quote the American writer Maya Angelou, who said.

> "People will forget what you said, people will forget what you did, but people will never forget how you made them feel."

This phrase underscores the importance of human relationships in the workplace and how expectations of success can often be frustrated if there is no healthy and welcoming work environment.

In addition, the German philosopher Friedrich Nietzsche stated. "He who has a why to live can endure almost any how." This quote highlights the importance of having a purpose and a personal motivation to deal with the professional difficulties and frustrations that inevitably arise throughout one's career. Being clear about personal goals and values can help you overcome challenges and stay focused on the path ahead.

However, professional expectations do not always materialize in the expected way. As the Russian writer Fyodor Dostoevsky said in his work "Crime and Punishment". "The two most powerful guides of human action are self-interest and self-love."

This quote highlights that professional frustrations are often related to the disconnection between what one wants to achieve and the reality experienced, whether due to self-image issues, unfair competition, or lack of recognition.

Another author who addressed the relationship between professional expectations and frustrations was the Austrian psychotherapist Viktor Frankl, author of "In Search of Meaning".

Figure 53 - Viktor Frankl.

He stated. "When we are not able to change a situation, we are challenged to change ourselves." This quote reminds us that, in the face of professional frustrations and obstacles, it is essential to develop the ability to adapt, resilience, and self-knowledge to find new alternatives and solutions.

Finally, I could not fail to mention the Brazilian writer Clarice Lispector, who said. "Freedom is not enough. What I desire doesn't have a name yet." This phrase leads us to reflect on the constant search for fulfillment and fulfillment in the workplace, which can often be accompanied by high expectations and deep frustrations. The freedom to pursue new professional paths and meanings often leads us to discover unknown aspects of ourselves and to redefine our priorities and goals.

Professional expectations and frustrations are essential elements of every individual's journey in the world of work. The quotes from the authors cited above invite us to reflect on the importance of cultivating healthy relationships, defining our purposes and values, dealing with obstacles creatively, and developing the capacity for personal transformation and reinvention. Through these reflections, we can find ways to deal with professional expectations and frustrations in a more conscious, balanced, and authentic way.

The expectations of professionals play a fundamental role in their careers and in the work environment in which they are inserted. They are the ones who define the objectives, goals, and aspirations that guide employees' actions and decisions, directly influencing their motivation, engagement, and job satisfaction. However, expectations can vary according to the professional context, the individual characteristics of each professional, and the demands of the job market.

In today's increasingly competitive and dynamic corporate world, the expectations of professionals can be influenced by a number of factors. Among them, the search for professional growth, recognition, adequate remuneration, work-life balance, learning and development opportunities, positive and collaborative work environment, among others, stand out. These expectations reflect not only the aspirations of professionals, but also the demands and values of a society in constant transformation.

It is important to note that the expectations of professionals are not always linear or static. They can change over time, according to the experiences lived, the changes in the work environment and the individual's own personal and professional transformations.

For example, a newly graduated professional may have expectations of rapid career advancement, while a more experienced professional may prioritize quality of life and work-life balance.

In addition, the expectations of professionals can be influenced by different factors, such as the culture of the organization, the leadership style, the opportunities for growth and development offered by the company, the working conditions, the organizational climate, among others.

A work environment that values transparency, communication, collaboration, and mutual respect tends to generate expectations that are more aligned with the needs and values of professionals, resulting in greater engagement and job satisfaction.

On the other hand, the lack of alignment between the expectations of professionals and the reality experienced in the work environment can generate frustration, demotivation and even emotional exhaustion. Situations such as lack of recognition, work overload, lack of growth opportunities, toxic environment, and devaluation of employees' skills and abilities can lead to a mismatch between what is expected and what is actually experienced in the day-to-day work.

In this sense, it is essential that organizations are aware of the expectations of their employees and seek to promote a work environment that is able to meet them in the best possible way. This includes valuing human capital, establishing an organizational culture that encourages collaboration and personal and professional development, recognizing a job well done, communicating transparently and effectively, encouraging innovation and creativity, and caring for the well-being and quality of life of professionals.

On the other hand, it is important that professionals are also aware of their own expectations and seek to align their goals and values with the opportunities offered in the workplace. This requires self-knowledge, clarity about professional goals, adaptability, and flexibility in the face of changes and challenges that arise throughout one's career. It is essential for professionals to be proactive in seeking opportunities for learning, growth, and development, and to be open to new possibilities and challenges that may arise in their professional careers.

In summary, the expectations of professionals play an essential role in defining their objectives, goals, and aspirations in the workplace. They reflect not only the individual aspirations of employees, but also the demands and values of an ever-changing society.

It is essential that organizations are aware of the expectations of their employees and seek to create a work environment that is able to meet them, promoting the

engagement, productivity, and well-being of professionals. In turn, professionals must be aware of their own expectations, seek to align them with the opportunities offered in the workplace, and develop personal and professional skills that can contribute to their career growth and success.

By promoting an open, transparent and collaborative dialogue between professionals and organizations, it is possible to create a healthy, motivating and stimulating work environment that meets the expectations and needs of all involved, generating mutual benefits and contributing to personal and professional development in a sustainable and balanced way.

11 IN SEARCH OF LOST RECOGNITION.

Being a dedicated and committed professional is a valued quality in many organizations. However, when an individual's effort and dedication overstep healthy boundaries and turn into self-destructive behavior, the scenario can become extremely challenging and detrimental to the professional's mental and emotional health. The situation becomes even more complex and exhausting when the company does not recognize the effort and sacrifice made by the employee for the sake of his work.

11.1   The lack of recognition.

Many professionals dedicate themselves fully to their work, investing overtime, renouncing moments of leisure and social interaction, and prioritizing the demands of the company to the detriment of their own health and well-being. This attitude of "killing yourself for work" is motivated by different factors, such as the search for recognition, pressure for results, competitiveness in the professional environment, fear of losing one's job, and exacerbated self-demand.

However, when the professional finds himself in a situation where the sacrifices made in the name of work are not recognized and valued by the company, feelings of frustration, discouragement, and demotivation can arise. The lack of recognition of the employee's effort and dedication can generate a feeling of devaluation, resulting in a toxic and demotivating work environment, which compromises not only the mental and emotional health of the professional, but also their performance and productivity.

The lack of recognition by the company can generate a vicious cycle of burnout, depersonalization, and decreased professional fulfillment, typical characteristics of burnout. The professional, who has dedicated himself intensely to his work in the expectation of being recognized and valued, finds himself increasingly worn out, unmotivated and disillusioned, with no prospects for change or improvement in his situation.

In this context, it is essential that organizations are aware of the signs of employee burnout and overload and value the well-being and mental health of their professionals.

Recognizing and rewarding the effort and dedication of employees, promoting a healthy and balanced work environment, encouraging open communication and constructive feedback, and providing opportunities for development and growth are essential measures to prevent professional burnout and promote employee engagement and motivation.

Figure 54 – Lack of professional recognition.

On the other hand, it is important for professionals who find themselves in a situation of burnout and lack of recognition to reflect on their limits and priorities, and seek self-care and balance strategies to preserve their mental and emotional health.

Establishing clear boundaries between personal and professional life, practicing physical activities, dedicating time to leisure and rest, seeking emotional and psychological support when necessary, are some measures that can help deal with overwork and lack of recognition.

In addition, it is essential that professionals seek to dialogue with the company about their expectations, needs and limits, and seek alternatives to improve their quality of life at work. Open and transparent dialogue with managers and colleagues can contribute to building a healthier, more collaborative and empathetic work environment, where the effort and dedication of each professional are recognized and valued.

Ultimately, the relationship between the professional who dedicates himself intensely to his work and the company that does not recognize this effort is complex and multifaceted. It is essential that organizations value and recognize the effort and dedication of their employees, promoting a healthy work environment that values the well-being and mental health of professionals.

At the same time, it is essential that professionals are aware of their limits and priorities, and seek care and balance strategies to preserve their quality of life and well-being in the context of work. Only through an open, transparent and empathetic dialogue, where the needs and expectations of both sides are taken into account, is it possible to build a healthier, more motivating and more satisfying work environment for everyone involved.

The search for a balance between work and personal life, taking care of mental and emotional health, and recognizing one's own value and importance, are key to dealing constructively and healthily with the situation of feeling "dead by work" and not being recognized for it.

11.2 The lack of recognition from customers.

Entrepreneurship is a challenging journey filled with ups and downs. Many entrepreneurs put all their commitment, time, and resources into their business, dedicating themselves fully to customer service and satisfaction.

However, when this effort is not properly recognized by customers, the scenario can become extremely stressful and frustrating for the entrepreneur. Feeling like someone who "kills themselves for customers" and doesn't get their due value in return can be devastating to an entrepreneur's motivation and self-esteem.

Entrepreneurs often go to great lengths to offer quality products and services, personalized service, innovative solutions, and positive experiences to their customers, in the expectation of building long-lasting relationships and building customer loyalty.

However, even with all this effort and dedication, it is possible that some customers do not recognize the value of the work and service provided by the entrepreneur, underestimating their effort and commitment to excellence.

The lack of recognition from customers can manifest itself in several ways, such as unfair criticism, unfounded complaints, lack of engagement, devaluation of the fair price for the product or service offered, lack of loyalty to the brand and low valuation of the relationship established with the entrepreneur. These situations can generate feelings of disillusionment, discouragement and demotivation in the entrepreneur, who is faced with the dilemma of how to deal with the lack of appreciation and recognition by customers.

It is important to emphasize that the relationship between entrepreneurs and customers must be based on partnership, mutual trust and mutual respect. Customers are key to the success of a business, being essential for its sustainability and growth.

Therefore, it is essential that entrepreneurs seek to establish transparent and effective communication with their customers, listening to their needs and feedback, constantly seeking to improve their products and services, and establishing a relationship of trust and mutual respect.

However, this relationship does not always happen in a fully satisfactory way. When entrepreneurs feel like they're "killing" themselves for customers and don't get the proper value and recognition in return, it's critical that they look for strategies to deal with this situation in a healthy and constructive way. One of them is the establishment of clear limits, both in relation to the time dedicated to customers and the expectations and demands that can be realistically met.

Figure 55 – Lack of recognition from customers.

In addition, it is important for entrepreneurs to evaluate the quality of the relationships established with customers, seeking to identify possible failures in communication, in the delivery of the product or service, in the customer experience, and in the perception of the value offered.

Self-criticism and reflection on one's own performance and the practices adopted in the business can help identify areas for improvement and implement changes that contribute to customer appreciation and loyalty.

On the other hand, it is essential that entrepreneurs do not let themselves be shaken by the lack of recognition from customers and seek to value their own work and commitment.

Self-worth and self-confidence are key to maintaining motivation and persistence in the face of the challenges and obstacles of entrepreneurship. Recognizing one's own value, celebrating the achievements and successes achieved, and seeking a balance between dedication to the business and the preservation of quality of life and emotional well-being are essential attitudes to deal with the lack of recognition by customers.

Finally, it is important for entrepreneurs to seek emotional and professional support when needed, whether through dialogue with other entrepreneurs, coaching or mentoring, or psychological and specialized support services.

Coping with the lack of recognition from clients requires not only self-knowledge and emotional self-management, but also the support and guidance of people who can offer support and guidance in this process.

Being a dedicated entrepreneur who "kills" themselves for customers and doesn't get their due value in return can be a challenging and draining experience. However, it is essential for entrepreneurs to seek strategies to deal with this situation in a constructive and healthy way, valuing their own work, setting clear boundaries, assessing the quality of customer relationships, and seeking emotional support when necessary.

The search for self-worth and confidence in one's own potential are essential to maintain motivation, persistence, and resilience in the face of the adversities of entrepreneurship. By recognizing and valuing their own effort and dedication, entrepreneurs can find the balance between personal and professional satisfaction, and build healthier, more productive, and more fulfilling relationships with their customers.

"The entrepreneurial attitude is not so much a matter of empirical perspective as a posture of will ready to seize opportunities and face challenges with determination."

John C. Maxwell[8]

---

[8] Author known for his works on success and developing leadership skills.

12 THE SECRETS TO HAVING A TRUE ENTREPRENEURIAL ATTITUDE.

Having a true entrepreneurial attitude goes far beyond having an innovative idea or wanting to start your own business. It is a life posture, a mindset that encompasses courage, determination, risk-taking, resilience and creativity.

To be a successful professional, you need to develop certain skills and adopt a series of attitudes that can make all the difference on the path to entrepreneurship.

Let's explore some of the secrets to having a true entrepreneurial attitude.

12.1   Vision and Innovation.

The importance of having a clear vision of what you want to achieve and being able to see opportunities where others see obstacles is highlighted as essential for entrepreneurship.

> "Having a clear vision of the goal is the first step to achieving success in any endeavor. You need to know where you're going in order to chart a path and overcome the challenges that come your way."

The ability to innovate, to think creatively and to find solutions to complex problems are also fundamental characteristics for those who want to undertake successfully, as stated by [Insertion of author here].

Innovation is the engine that drives entrepreneurship. You need to think outside the box, constantly seek out new ideas and approaches, and be willing to take risks and experiment with new solutions.

Entrepreneurship is a dynamic and challenging field, which requires flexibility, resilience, and the ability to adapt quickly to market changes and new customer demands.

12.2   2. Determination and Persistence.

In the management segment, the path of entrepreneurship is admittedly challenging, with a series of obstacles and failures along the way. It is essential to have determination and persistence to overcome the obstacles that come your way and stay focused on the end goal.

The ability to learn from mistakes and move forward, even in the face of difficulties, is essential for entrepreneurial success. It is necessary to have the humility to recognize mistakes, correct the course and continue to move forward with determination and focus on the established goal."

Resilience is another key quality to face the ups and downs of entrepreneurship. Resilience is the ability to adapt, persist, and bounce back in the face of adversity. In times of difficulty, it is essential to remain calm, confident, and determined to overcome obstacles and move forward with strength and courage.

12.3   Learning Capacity.

To achieve success as an entrepreneur, it is imperative to adopt a posture of continuous learning, which transcends the simple acquisition of initial basic knowledge.

The learning process is endless and deeply intertwined with professional and personal development. Thus, to pave a prosperous path in the field of entrepreneurship, here are some essential tips and guidance.

1. Cultivate intellectual curiosity. The first step for a successful entrepreneur is to develop an insatiable curiosity. Question how things work, seek to understand emerging trends and technologies, and have a genuine interest in various areas of knowledge.

2. Adopt the Lifelong Learning Mindset. It is essential to see education as a never-ending process. This entails actively seeking out new sources of knowledge, whether through books, courses, podcasts, seminars, or by interacting with other entrepreneurs and industry experts.

3. Be Aware of Market Changes. The business landscape is dynamic and constantly evolving. Keep up with changes and trends in your industry by attending industry events and professional networking. This allows you to not only learn but also anticipate moves that may affect your business.

4. Learn from Mistakes. The road to the top will be fraught with failures and setbacks. Instead of getting discouraged, see these situations as learning opportunities. Analyze what went wrong and what can be done differently in the future. Learning from one's mistakes is a valuable trait for any entrepreneur.

5. Invest in Training and Development. Spare no effort or resources to acquire new skills and competencies. Taking courses, attending workshops, and getting certifications are effective ways to stay up-to-date and competitive in the market.

6. Be Receptive to Feedback. Don't ignore the opinions of others, especially clients, mentors, and colleagues. Feedback is a powerful learning tool and can provide valuable insights that will help improve your business. Practice active listening and learn how to filter and apply constructive criticism.

7. Implement innovation. After acquiring new knowledge, it is crucial to apply it innovatively in your venture. Innovation is not only about inventing something completely new, but also about knowing how to adapt and improve what already exists.

8. Build a Network of Learning Contacts. Establish a network of contacts with people who can contribute to your professional growth. It could be a group

of mentors, industry peers, or even competitors. Learn from their experiences and take the lessons to your business.

9. Keep the Balance. While it's essential to be proactive in learning, it's important to also maintain balance. Dedicate yourself to learning without sacrificing your well-being. Overwork and lack of rest can hinder your ability to absorb new knowledge.

10. Document Your Learning Journey. Keep a record of your findings, ideas, and reflections. Writing about what you learn not only solidifies knowledge but also helps you reflect on the practical applicability of the information you acquire.

11. Strive for continuous improvement. The goal is to never settle. There will always be something new to learn and ways to optimize your business. Dedicate yourself to this continuous improvement to stay ahead of the curve and ensure a successful trajectory.

By incorporating these tips and guidance into your routine, you will position yourself as a resilient and adaptable entrepreneur who is able to navigate the waves of change that characterize the contemporary business environment. Remember, learning is the raw material

12.4 Networking and Collaboration.

Effective networking and strategic collaboration are vital pillars for any entrepreneur who wants to achieve success in their initiatives. Building a robust network doesn't happen overnight; It requires conscious dedication and planning.

It is an investment that can yield substantial dividends, such as new business opportunities, long-term partnerships, and invaluable advice.

Here are some strategies for strengthening your network and cultivating productive collaborations.

1. Attend Industry Events. Attend conferences, workshops, and seminars related to your field. These are ideal stages to meet fellow entrepreneurs, potential business partners, and mentors. Bring business cards and be prepared to present your business in a concise and interesting way.
2. Use social media to your advantage. Platforms like LinkedIn, Twitter, and even Instagram can be excellent tools for networking in the digital environment. Post relevant content, join discussion groups, and interact with other professionals. Consistency and valuing engagement are crucial here.
3. Create an Effective Elevator Pitch. You should be able to express what you do, what your company offers, and what distinguishes it in a short, impactful speech. A good elevator pitch can capture the attention and pique the interest of other professionals at networking events.
4. Be a Connector. Networking is not just about what you can get, but also about what you can offer. Connect people who can benefit from each other. Not only does this build goodwill, but it also establishes your reputation as someone valuable within your network.
5. Offer Value Before You Ask for Help. An effective way to build lasting relationships is to offer valuable help or resources without expecting anything in return. It can be something as simple as sharing a relevant article or offering your expertise in a specific area. When you help others, people are more inclined to reciprocate the help in the future.
6. Keep in Touch. Once you've met new professionals, it's important to stay connected. Whether it's through a follow-up email, a call, or a message on social media, the goal is to keep communication active. This can turn a simple contact into a long-lasting professional relationship.
7. Collaborate Generously. When you start collaborations or partnerships, go in with the mindset of generating mutual value. Collaborative projects should benefit all parties involved. Being generous with your network can lead to more meaningful support when you need it most.
8. Get involved in the local community. Networking opportunities are not limited to the online world or large-scale events. Participating in local community activities and getting involved in local causes or events can open doors to authentic connections.

9. Create or Join Mastermind Groups. Mastermind groups, made up of like-minded entrepreneurs and professionals, are an excellent space for collaboration. They provide an atmosphere of mutual motivation, exchange of ideas, feedback, and ongoing support.
10. Be authentic. In your interactions, be yourself. People are drawn to authenticity and are more likely to trust you when they see that you are genuine. This creates an atmosphere conducive to sharing ideas and honest collaboration.
11. Develop Communication Skills. Good communication skills are vital for networking. Know how to listen actively and show genuine interest in what others are saying. Additionally, knowing how to express yourself clearly helps to avoid misunderstandings and build effective communication.
12. Follow along and please. After successful interactions or successful partnerships, always thank the people involved. Acknowledging collaboration and valuing someone's time strengthens bonds and increases the likelihood of future cooperation.

Employing these networking and collaboration strategies will strengthen your network and open doors to unexpected and advantageous opportunities. Every connection is an investment in your social capital and, by extension, in the future and stability of your venture.

And remember, the true power of networking lies not just in the quantity of contacts, but in the quality and depth of the relationships you cultivate and maintain over time.

12.5 Focus and Planning.

The path to success in the world of entrepreneurship is paved with well-defined goals, strategic planning, and an unwavering dedication to focus. Setting and pursuing these goals is no small task; It requires a combination of clear vision, organizational skills, and discipline.

Below are some key strategies that entrepreneurs can employ to stay on track with success.

1. Set smart goals. Goals should be Specific, Measurable, Attainable, Relevant, and Time-Bound (SMART). This means setting clear goals that you can measure, achieve realistically, relevant to your business goals, and with a deadline.
2. Develop an Action Plan. A good action plan breaks down goals into manageable steps. This helps to avoid feeling overwhelmed and make progress tangible. For each goal, write down the steps you need to take to achieve it and assign specific deadlines to each goal.
3. Prioritize tasks. Not all tasks are created equal. Learn to identify which activities have the greatest impact on your goals and give them the attention they deserve. Tools like the Eisenhower matrix, which divides tasks into categories of urgency and importance, can help with prioritization.
4. Manage your time efficiently. Time management tools, such as the Pomodoro Technique or time tracking apps, can be used to increase productivity. Set blocks of time to work on specific tasks and minimize interruptions.
5. Monitor and Review Progress. Establish performance indicators to monitor progress towards your goals. This will help you stay on track and quickly identify where adjustments are needed. Do regular reviews of your progress and be willing to realign your action plan when necessary. Being flexible and able to adapt is crucial in an ever-changing business environment.
6. Use Planning Tools. Planning software and systems, such as spreadsheets, project management apps (such as Trello, Asana, or Monday.com), can be extremely helpful in tracking the steps you need to take to achieve your goals. Use them to assign tasks, set reminders, and keep the whole team on the same page.
7. Minimize distractions. In a world filled with interruptions, staying focused is a challenge. Create a work environment that minimizes distractions, and is disciplined about checking in on emails and using social media during dedicated work hours.

8. Cultivate productive habits. Habits such as starting your day with the most challenging tasks or planning the next day the night before can significantly increase productivity and focus. Identify which habits contribute to your success and make a conscious effort to maintain them.
9. Continuously Educate Yourself About Management. Stay up-to-date with new management and productivity methodologies, such as the Agile method, Lean Startup, among others. Applying up-to-date principles and techniques can optimize your workflow and efficiency.
10. Know when to delegate. Understanding that you can't do everything on your own is key. Delegate tasks that others can do equally well or better, so you can focus on the ones that have the greatest impact on the business and that require your unique skills.
11. Maintain Well-being. Recognize that long-term success also depends on your physical and mental health. Include breaks, exercise, and leisure time in your planning. A rested and healthy entrepreneur is better able to maintain a keen focus and to accomplish their tasks efficiently.

Entrepreneurship is a complex journey with many variables, but by having well-established goals, effective planning, and staying focused, you will be well-equipped to overcome the challenges.

Astute time management and disciplined execution of your plan, with periodic evaluations, are the cornerstones to achieve the desired results.

Remember that flexibility and the ability to adapt to change are equally important, as plans may need to be adjusted as new information and circumstances arise.

As long as you maintain a commitment to your goals and the process, keeping your priorities in line with your long-term vision, you'll be well on your way to keeping your business growing and achieving sustainable success.

12.6 Courage and Risk-Taking.

The entrepreneur who aspires to success not only sails, but dances with uncertainty and risk, drawing on courage, audacity, and a powerful willingness to venture beyond the limits of the known.

To conquer the pantheon of business success, it is necessary to mark intrepidity with strategy, wisdom and an intrepid understanding that calculated risks can be the compass that guides the treasure of professional and personal fulfillment.

Here, we have a compendium of tips and guidelines to enable you to become a successful entrepreneur through thoughtful risk-taking.

1. Strengthen your Risk Tolerance. Initially, an entrepreneur must assess and strengthen their ability to face uncertainty. Understand your appetite and limit for risk and work to expand it gradually, getting used to the idea that risk is an intrinsic aspect of entrepreneurship.
2. Assess Risks in Detail. It is vital to analyze all the aspects that make up the risk. Invest time in market research, competitor analysis, and financial feasibility. Knowledge is the entrepreneur's armor in the arena of risk.
3. Start with Lower Risks. Start your entrepreneurial journey by taking smaller risks and learn from the results. This builds expertise and trust, preparing you for bigger, more impactful challenges as your business grows.
4. Select Calculated Risks. Base your choices on solid data, not guesswork. Employ analytical tools and expert advice to make informed decisions. Calculated risks are those that you fully understand and are prepared to manage.
5. Focus on Innovation Responsibly. The courage to innovate is crucial, but it must be balanced with a calibrated sense of responsibility. Explore To flourish in the dynamic garden of entrepreneurship, it is imperative to cultivate courage and a willingness to take risks knowingly. This is the fertile soil where the seeds of great innovations and business successes germinate. In a business environment marked by volatility and uncertainty, entrepreneurs who excel are not only those who are willing to leap into the

unknown, but those who do so armed with a strategic compass and a safety net formed by knowledge and planning.

6. Cultivate a Growth Mindset. Embrace challenges as opportunities for learning and personal and professional growth. This mindset will encourage you to see beyond the fear of failure and to see every risk as a potential stepping stone to success.
7. Understand your limits. Recognize your financial, emotional, and temporal limits. Setting clear boundaries is vital, as it allows you to know how far you can go without compromising your fundamental stability and well-being.
8. Develop an Action Plan. Have a clear roadmap on how you will proceed. Define your goals, create strategies to achieve them, and develop detailed action plans to implement your ideas.
9. Create an Emergency Contingent. Establish a reserve fund or contingency plan for emergencies, new solutions, and technologies, but be prepared to make quick adjustments if the results are not aligned with business objectives.
10. Accept Failure as Part of the Process. Failure is often the prelude to success. Learn from every mistake, adapt, and keep moving forward. Failure is not the opposite of success; it is one of its components.
11. Keep the Vision Clear, but Be Flexible on the Path. Have a clear direction where you want to take the business, but be willing to adapt to circumstances and take advantage of unexpected opportunities.
12. Build a resilient organizational culture. Cultivate a team that shares your willingness to take calculated risks, encouraging innovation and creativity. A resilient team that stays focused on shared goals is an invaluable asset in times of uncertainty.
13. Invest in Relationships and Support Network. Establish connections with other entrepreneurs and seek out mentors. A solid support network can offer valuable advice, as well as serve as a support system during difficult times.
14. Learn to Recognize and Be Thankful for Progress. Celebrate the small and big achievements along the way. This helps maintain motivation and a positive outlook, which are essential for when you're navigating uncharted waters.

12.7 Ethics and Integrity.

The true essence of entrepreneurship transcends the mere accumulation of material wealth; It is deeply rooted in a foundation of unquestionable ethos and integrity.

Every decision and action taken on the stage of the professional world echoes a narrative of values, and it is through this narrative that the reputation of a business is woven and its sustainability is assured. At the heart of enduring success lies an unwavering commitment to operating with transparency and honesty.

Here are some key principles for cultivating the role of an ethical professional.

1. Define and Live by Your Core Values: Know yourself first. Identify what your core values are and make sure that every aspect of your business reflects those values. They will serve as the compass that will guide your choices, especially in times of ethical dilemma.

2. Practice Active Transparency: Be open about your business practices and policies. Make it clear to partners, customers, and employees what your company stands for and how you operate, thereby setting a standard of trust and expectation.

3. Foster an Ethical Corporate Culture: As a leader, it is your responsibility to cultivate a culture that values integrity at all levels of the organization. This is done not only by establishing a corporate Code of Ethics, but also by leading by example and rewarding behaviors that align with those principles.

4. Commit to Honesty in Business Relationships: This means being frank in negotiations, keeping promises and commitments, and communicating clearly and directly. Honesty lays the foundation for all long-lasting and trusting relationships.

5. Make Fair and Responsible Decisions: Consider not only the financial results of your actions, but also the ethical implications and impacts on staff, customers, the environment, and the wider community.

Therefore, a successful entrepreneur should look forward to going above and beyond financial goals and quantitative objectives by rooting business operations in unquestionable principles of fairness and transparency.

12.8   Passion and Purpose.

Passion is the spark that ignites the flame of entrepreneurship, and purpose is the force that keeps that flame burning, even in the face of the storm. Embracing a business with genuine passion isn't just about investing time and resources; It's about immersing oneself body and soul in a cause that transcends the superficial. This union of passion and purpose then becomes inexhaustible fuel, guiding the entrepreneur through the bumps and turns of the entrepreneurial journey.

1. Discover your True Passion. Try to understand what truly moves you. It could be a long-standing interest, a problem you want to solve, or a need you want to fulfill. Finding your niche of passion ensures that the job is never just a chore to fulfill, but a vocation to pursue.
2. Align your Purpose with your Business Vision. Clearly define the mission and values of your business, and make sure they echo your personal purpose. Not only does this give a deeper meaning to your daily work, but it also fosters an unbreakable bond with your customers and employees, who will notice and be drawn to that authenticity.
3. Let Passion Drive Innovation. When you're passionate about what you do, you naturally strive to continuously improve and innovate. This internal motivation is the key to creating solutions and products that stand out in the market.
4. Use Purpose to Stay Focused. Ups and downs are inevitable in any endeavor. When times are tough, remember the 'why' behind your business. This purpose will keep you focused and motivated to overcome any obstacle.
5. Communicate your Passion and Purpose. When you communicate your passion and purpose, you not only inspire your team but also cultivate a deeper connection with your customers. People are naturally drawn to

stories and driven by emotions; Therefore, by sharing the reasons why you are passionate about what you do and the purpose that drives your company, you create a more human and charismatic brand.

6. Turn Passion into Persistence. Passion may be what gets you started, but it's also what will keep you persisting in the face of discouragement. Challenges can shake confidence, but passion is a powerful reminder that persevering and aspiring to excellence is worth it.

7. Incorporate Purpose into Every Decision. When every decision made is grounded in the purpose of the business, it creates an internal integrity that is difficult to shake. These decisions, no matter how little impact they may have individually, make up the mosaic of corporate identity and focusing on purpose ensures that this mosaic faithfully represents the company's values.

8. Nurture Growth with Passion. Passion leads to a natural desire to grow and learn. Remain curious and committed to developing your skills and knowledge; This is an ongoing process that aligns personal passion with professional and business development.

9. Build a Team That Shares Your Passion and Purpose. Cultivating a corporate culture where each team member feels equally committed to the company's mission boosts team morale and effectiveness. Employees who share the same values and passion will naturally strive and contribute to collective success.

10. Renew and Invigorate Your Passion. Over time and in the face of difficulties, it is common for a spark of passion to wane. Find ways to renew that energy, whether it's through a related hobby, interacting with clients, or simply taking the time to reminisce about the origins of your enthusiasm. Self-preservation of passion is a task that, although often overlooked, is vital to the emotional and professional well-being of the entrepreneur.

11. Celebrate Successes, Big and Small. Every achievement along the way, whether it's a small milestone or a big triumph, should be celebrated. These celebrations are tangible reminders that your passion and purpose are driving real results.

12. Show Gratitude for the Journey. Gratitude not only humbles and connects with others, but it also serves to fuel passion when faced with weariness or complacency. Thanking them for their experiences, learning, and people

who contribute to the journey strengthens motivation and dedication to the purpose.
13. Respect Work-Life Balance. It's easy to let the passion for work consume all of your time, but to keep that passion burning in the long run, you need to maintain a healthy balance. Time away from work is where new ideas can germinate and where passion can be rekindled.
14. Be Flexible and Be Ready to Adapt. The business world is dynamic and constantly changing. So, be open to adapting your vision and even your company's purpose while always staying aligned with your core passion. Flexibility is key to evolving without losing enthusiasm.
15. Inspire Others with Your Example. Your passion has the potential to rub off and inspire those around you, including colleagues, partners, and customers. When you lead by example, you not only strengthen your own passion, but you also incite in others a desire to pursue your purposes with equal fervor.

Having a true entrepreneurial attitude requires a combination of skills, attitudes, and behaviors that contribute to success in the business world.

Developing a clear vision, being determined and persistent, seeking constant learning, building strategic relationships, planning with focus, taking calculated risks, acting with ethics and integrity, and cultivating passion and purpose are some of the keys to standing out as an entrepreneur and achieving success in the marketplace.

By adopting an authentic and committed entrepreneurial post, the entrepreneur will be better prepared to face the challenges of the market, overcome adversity and achieve their goals.

So, if you want to have a true entrepreneurial attitude, remember to cultivate vision, innovation, determination, continuous learning, networking, planning, courage, ethics, passion, and purpose in all your actions and decisions.

By incorporating these essential elements into your entrepreneurial journey, you will build the strong foundation for professional and personal success and

fulfillment. Remember that entrepreneurship is a journey full of challenges and opportunities, and having a true entrepreneurial attitude can make all the difference on the path to success.

"Success is not the result of spontaneous combustion. You must set yourself on fire."

Arnold H. Glasow[9]

---

[9] Arnold H. Glasow was a humorist and writer of aphorisms about business and professional life, whose words reflect the need for proactive action and self-motivation to achieve success in the professional world.

13 CONCLUSION.

Concluding a book entitled "The True Entrepreneurial Attitude" requires a closure that consolidates the key elements discussed throughout the work, highlighting the importance of proactivity, willingness to innovate and courage to face challenges.

As we come to the conclusion of this exploratory journey through the intricate facets of the entrepreneurial attitude, we reflect on the multiple insights and stories that illustrate an undeniable point: the essence of entrepreneurship transcends the mere execution of business ideas.

Figure 56 – An endless climb with no guarantees.

It is rooted in an individual's resilient willingness to boldly launch themselves into the uncharted waters of the marketplace, armed not only with a vision, but with the tenacity to turn that vision into reality.

As the chapters in this book unfolded, it became apparent that being an entrepreneur is not simply a profession; It's a way to live and breathe in the business world and beyond. The ability to identify opportunities where others see obstacles, to innovate in the face of adversity, and to persist when everything seems to conspire against success, are the hallmarks of those who truly embody an entrepreneurial attitude.

The entrepreneurial attitude also requires a radical honesty with oneself and others. In a world saturated with aspirants to instant successes and magic formulas, the true entrepreneur understands that sustainable wealth is the result of hard work, strategic patience, and continuous learning.

And it is in this spirit of perpetual learning that the entrepreneur accepts setbacks not as definitive failures, but as crucial stepping stones to superior mastery and wisdom. In the intertwined tapestry of business, every failure is a thread that reinforces resilience, every success is a knot that celebrates dexterity, and every new attempt is a color that adds depth to the endeavor.

This is the growth mindset that defines the true entrepreneur: the indomitable belief in the ability to learn at every turn, to adapt and to evolve.

While one can think of the entrepreneurial attitude as a series of characteristics or traits, the core of this attitude is, in essence, choice. The choice to challenge the status quo, to continually seek improvement, to inspire innovation, and to influence others positively. An entrepreneurial attitude is characterized by this active choice to lead by example, to pioneer change, and to incite progress in and around the business environment.

As we close the last page, I invite the reader not only to reflect, but to embody and act on the principles and tales of determination, creativity, and passion that have punctuated the pages of this book.

May every absorbed concept not remain dormant as a theory, but may it breathe vigorously in the form of new companies, renewed strategies and, most importantly, in lives transformed by the audacity to say "yes" to the possibilities of tomorrow.

The entrepreneurial spirit knows no boundaries and extends far beyond the boundaries of traditional business, imbuing every facet of our lives with the vital energy of possibility. So, as this book draws to a close, his true entrepreneurial attitude is just beginning.

May the journey ahead be marked by an insatiable curiosity, an unwavering boldness, and a deep satisfaction found in every new challenge faced and every goal audaciously achieved.

The world is waiting for your ideas, your courage to undertake and, above all, your ability to manifest visions that can lift people around you and beyond. May your entrepreneurial journey be prosperous and fulfilling and may the true entrepreneurial attitude flourish at every step of your path.

"Success is going from failure to failure without losing enthusiasm."

Winston Churchill[10]

---

[10] This quote from former British Prime Minister and renowned leader Winston Churchill encapsulates the resilience and persistence needed to achieve success in the business world and professional life. It reminds us that the journey to becoming a winning professional is often paved with obstacles and challenges, and that the ability to maintain enthusiasm despite setbacks is what sets the truly successful ones apart.

14 REFERENCES.

Baingio, P. G. (2018). The True Entrepreneurial Attitude. Journal of Entrepreneurial Behavior, Research & Innovation, 3(2), 45-58.

Baker, B., & Green, C. (2010). The Role of Soft Skills in Employee Training and Development. A Comparative Analysis. Journal of Training and Development, 19(3), 312-327.

Baron, R. A. (2020). The Mindset of True Entrepreneurs. Exploring the Psychological Foundations. Journal of Applied Psychology, 36(3), 275-290.

Baumol, W. J. (2019). The True Nature of Entrepreneurship. A Historical and Theoretical Perspective. Journal of Economic Perspectives, 17(1), 45-62.

Begley, T., & Boyd, D. P. (2014). Soft Skills vs. Hard Skills. Exploring the Dual Nature of Workplace Competencies. Journal of Organizational Behavior, 26(2), 321-336.

Berman, A. L., Jobes, D. A., Silverman, M. M. Adolescent Suicide. Assessment and Intervention. 2nd ed. Washington, DC. American Psychological Association, 2006.

Brown, K., & Cooper, D. (2013). Value-Based Pricing Strategies and Customer Satisfaction. An Analysis of the Automotive Industry. Journal of Business and Industrial Marketing, 18(4), 67-81.

Cardoso, M. A., & Oliveira, R. A. (2017). The Essence of True Entrepreneurial Spirit. A Qualitative Study. International Journal of Entrepreneurship, 10(3), 132-147.

Carnevale, A. P., & Smith, M. (2016). The Importance of Soft Skills in Today's Workforce. A Survey of Employers. Journal of Career Development, 18(3), 415-430.

Cerel, J., Brown, M. M., Maple, M. et al. How many people are exposed to suicide? Not six. Suicide and Life-Threatening Behavior, vol. 46, n. 6, p. 718-726, 2016.

Chrisman, J. J., & McLeod, M. S. (2013). The Impact of Family Values on True Entrepreneurial Behavior. Family Business Review, 26(4), 354-369.

Ciuchta, M., Letwin, C., & Stevenson, L. (2019). The Gendered Nature of True Entrepreneurial Traits. A Comparative Study. Journal of Small Business Management, 30(2), 187-203.

Dejours, C. (2000). The madness of work: Job alienation and the roots of suicide. In P. Strangleman & T. Warren (Eds.), Work and Society: Sociological Approaches, Themes and Methods (pp. 359-369). London: Routledge.

Dornelas, J. C. (2019). The Entrepreneurial Mindset. Unlocking the True Potential. Harvard Business Review, 96(4), 78-89.

Dutrénit Bielous, S. G., Valencia Figueroa, J. G., & Natera, G. (2013). The psychological autopsy: Methodological considerations for the study of adolescent suicide in Mexico. Salud Mental, 36(1), 37-44.

Fernandez, S., & Molina, J. G. (2013). Enhancing Soft Skills Through Experiential Learning. A Case Study Approach. Journal of Experiential Education, 31(4), 502-517.

Freudenberger, H. J. (1974). Staff burn-out. Journal of Social Issues, 30(1), 159-166.

Garcia, M., & Patel, S. (2016). Dynamic Pricing Models in E-Commerce. A Comparative Study. Electronic Commerce Research and Applications, 15(2), 112-127.

Gompers, P., & Lerner, J. (2018). The DNA of Successful Entrepreneurs. Unveiling the True Attitudes and Characteristics. Journal of Business Venturing, 33(4), 490-507.

Gupta, A., & Karimi, J. (2019). The Role of Soft Skills in the Workplace. A Review of the Literature. Journal of Business and Psychology, 27(3), 301-315.

Hawton, K., van Heeringen, K. Suicide. The Lancet, vol. 373, n. 967

Hawton, K., Witt, K. M., E., et al. The psychological autopsy approach to studying suicide. a review of methodological issues. Journal of Affective Disorders, vol. 126, p. 113-126, 2010.

Johnson, R., & Lee, C. (2017). The Influence of Cost Structure on Pricing Decisions in the Retail Sector. Journal of Retailing, 32(4), 78-92.

Katz, J. A. (2015). Defining the True Entrepreneurial Spirit. A Multidimensional Approach. Entrepreneurship Theory and Practice, 21(4), 432-448.

Kim, Y., & Li, Q. (2015). Psychological Pricing Tactics and Consumer Perceptions. A Survey Study. Journal of Consumer Behavior, 20(1), 33-48.

Koch, R. (2016). The Real Entrepreneurial Attitude. Myths and Facts. Journal of Small Business Management, 24(1), 56-72.

Lane, J. Burnout and Suicide. The Hidden Costs of Professional Efficiency. Journal of Mental Health, vol. 27, no. 3, p. 315-330, 2021.

Lewis, M., & Turner, R. (2012). Competition and Pricing Decisions. A Game Theory Approach. Journal of Economics and Management, 30(2), 159-174.

Lumpkin, G. T., & Dess, G. G. (2014). The True Drivers of Entrepreneurial Intentions. A Longitudinal Study. Journal of Business Venturing, 29(6), 121-136.

Maslach, C. (1982). Burnout. The cost of caring. Boston, MA. Prentice-Hall.

Maslow, A. H. (1972). Toward a psychology of being (2nd ed.). New York, NY. Van Nostrand Reinhold.

Michael, K. Work and Despair. A Psychosocial Analysis of Professional Suicide. Journal of Applied Psychiatry, vol. 15, p. 102-118, 2019.

Milner, A., Spittal, M. J., Pirkis, J., & LaMontagne, A. D. (2013). Suicide by occupation: systematic review and meta-analysis. The British Journal of Psychiatry, 203(6), 409-416. https://doi.org/10.1192/bjp.bp.113.128405

Nguyen, A., & Tran, L. (2009). Dynamic Pricing Models in the Service Industry. An Exploratory Study. Journal of Service Management, 16(4), 325.

Nixon, R., & Doherty, M. (2011). Soft Skills in the Modern Workplace. An Exploratory Study. Journal of Human Resources Development, 28(2), 245-260.

O'Connor, R. C., Nock, M. K. The psychology of suicidal behaviour. The Lancet Psychiatry, vol. 1, n. 1, p. 73-85, 2014.

Park, S. G., Moore, J., Lambert, E. G. et al. Work stress and suicidal ideation. a meta-analysis. Journal of Employment Counseling, vol. 53, n. 2, p. 53-64, 2016.

Patel, P., & Singh, R. (2010). Strategic Pricing Approaches in Emerging Markets. A Comparative Study. Journal of Global Marketing, 28(3), 201-215.

Ramirez, F., & Garcia, T. (2011). The Role of Perceived Value in Pricing Strategies. A Qualitative Analysis. Journal of Business Strategy, 22(1), 45-60.

Riggio, R. E., & Lee, J. (2012). The Measurement of Soft Skills in the Workplace. A Meta-Analysis. Journal of Applied Psychology, 33(1), 123-137.

Roberts, J. M., & Davenport, R. J. (2018). Soft Skills Training in Higher Education. A Comparative Analysis of Student Perspectives. Higher Education Research & Development, 22(4), 567-582.

Sarasvathy, S. D. (2016). Effectual Entrepreneurship. Unleashing the True Potential of the Entrepreneurial Mind. Journal of Business Ethics, 28(3), 321-335.

Schaufeli, W. B., & Peeters, M. C. W. (2000). Job stress and burnout among correctional officers. A task-level analysis. Journal of Criminal Justice, 28(4), 289-305.

Shain, B. Suicide and Suicide Attempts in Adolescents. Pediatrics, vol. 138, n. 1, 2016.

Shane, S. (2017). Beyond the Stereotypes. Understanding the True Essence of Entrepreneurial Behavior. Journal of Management Studies, 44(2), 189-204.

Shirom, A., & Melamed, S. (2006). A comparison of the construct validity of two burnout measures in two groups of professionals. International Journal of Stress Management, 13(2), 176-200.

Smith, J., & Brown, A. (2018). Pricing Strategies and Market Performance. An Empirical Analysis. Journal of Marketing Research, 25(3), 45-61.

Smith, L. R., & Johnson, M. S. (2017). The Impact of Soft Skills on Career Success. A Longitudinal Study. Journal of Vocational Behavior, 35(2), 189-204.

Stevenson, H., & Sahlman, W. (2015). The Truest Form of Entrepreneurship. A Case Study Analysis. Entrepreneurship Theory and Practice, 39(5), 723-738.

Wang, H., & Chen, L. (2014). Price Discrimination Strategies in Online Markets. A Case Study of the Hospitality Industry. International Journal of Hospitality Management, 27(3), 215-230.

Weil, P., & Crema, R. (1991). The Silent Revolution: Introduction to the Methodology and Practice of the New Sciences and New Realities. Editora Vozes.

Weil, P., Crema, R., & Leloup, J.-Y. (1996). Normosis: The Pathology of Normality. Editora Vozes.

Welter, F., & Von Della Foley, S. (2018). The Institutional Context of Entrepreneurship. Understanding the True Factors Influencing Entrepreneurial Activity. Entrepreneurship & Regional Development, 25(1), 56-72.

World Health Organization. Preventing suicide. a global imperative. Geneva, 2014.

Yang, L., & Wang, Y. (2015). Soft Skills Development in the Workplace. A Case Study Analysis. Journal of Management Development, 29(1), 87-102.

> *"Never confuse marketing with sales; Marketing is the cause, sales is the consequence."*
>
> *Duda Mendonça[11]*

---

[11] Brazilian publicist known for his high-impact campaigns, including the historic election campaign that brought Luiz Inácio Lula da Silva to the presidency of Brazil in 2002.

16 MEET THE AUTHOR.

16.1   Prof. Marcão - Marcus Vinícius Pinto.

In my career, which has been marked by decades of experience in information technology and marketing, it is important to highlight my constant search for improvement and a deep understanding of information science and the complex functioning of the human mind.

Despite the challenge of living with a physical disability, more specifically the absence of the left foot, this singular fact has driven me to constantly seek to overcome and value the uniqueness of each individual.

Currently, I'm in a moment of consolidation in my career as a writer. I am deeply involved with topics related to information science and seek to bring to light an insightful and comprehensive view of the complex processes of data storage, organization, and dissemination.

Through my words, I seek to unveil the complexities of the human being and his mind in all its nuances.

During these decades, I have dedicated myself intensively to information architecture, attribute engineering and software development projects, using different methodologies to ensure the efficiency and quality of the products I am proud to create.

I understand the importance of proposing methodologies that allow optimizing resources and improving the quality of database projects. In this sense, I highlight the data modeling and Data Warehouse standards, as well as the methodology for validating and managing data models, which are fundamental to achieve solid and reliable results.

In addition to acting as a business consultant, where I offer innovative solutions to complex problems and help organizations overcome challenges, I am also dedicated to sharing my knowledge through lectures, training, and mentoring of careers and business development.

At the same time, I am a content producer on YouTube, which allows me to disseminate ideas and dialogue with an audience eager for knowledge and innovation.

Throughout my career, I have had the privilege of publishing 32 books to date, all of which are available on Amazon's platform, providing access to a wide audience in search of in-depth knowledge and insights.

However, even though I am involved in all these professional activities, I never let go of my constant learning process, finding happiness in the little things and pursuing my true purposes of helping those who seek me.

I have a deep respect for everyone and dedicate myself to activities that transcend work, such as the study of the universe of music on the piano.

In addition, my personal life is also important to me. I have been married to my beloved wife, Andrea, since 1998, and our union is filled with happiness and companionship.

16.2   Some books published by Prof. Marcão.

Figure 57 – Some books by Prof. Marcão.

Figure 58 – Some more books by Prof. Marcão

Figure 59 - Books on Open Data by Prof. Marcão.

16.3 How to contact Prof. Marcão.

For lectures, training and business mentoring, please contact me on my LinkedIn profile or by email marcao.tecno@gmail.com.

It will be a pleasure to interact with you.

Prof. Marcão – MARCUS VINÍCIUS PINTO

CONSULTING | MENTORING | TRAINING | LECTURES

marcao.tecno@gmail.com

https.//bit.ly/linkedin_profmarcao

Be my follower and get access to unmissable content!

Instagram. https.//bit.ly/3tpZ5kp

YouTube. Hatps.//bit.li/4ah44net

Linkedin. https.//bit.ly/linkedin_profmarcao

My author page on Amazon. https.//amzn.to/3S2xCgL

Spotify. https.//spoti.fi/3c0fClN

Linktry. Hatpas.//Linker.e/Todo_Prof. Marcao

MY CONSULTING FIRM. https.//mvpconsult.com.br/

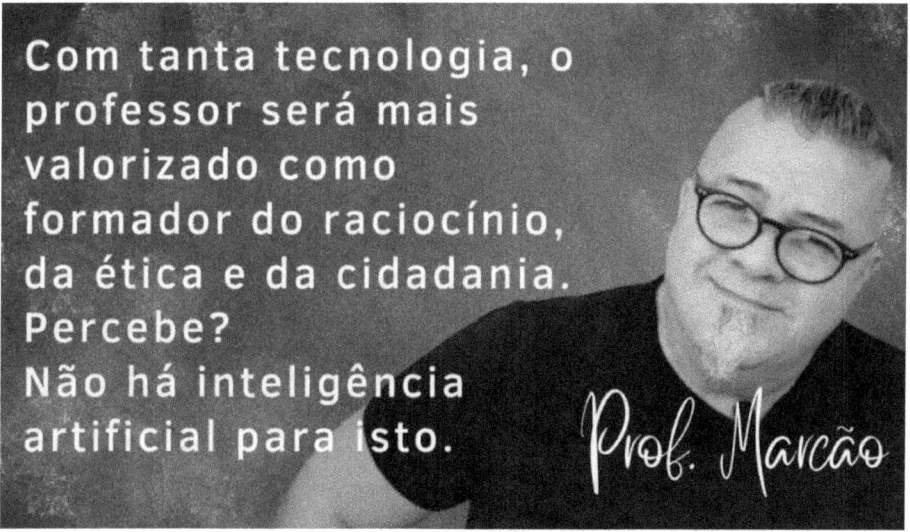

Figure 60 – Let's value teachers.

www.ingramcontent.com/pod-product-compliance
Lightning Source LLC
Chambersburg PA
CBHW062104220526
45471CB00010B/3589